"YOU SHALL GO OUT WITH JOY . . ."

. . . into Congo and Zambia

By

Robert Muir

JOHN RITCHIE LTD
CHRISTIAN PUBLICATIONS

40 Beansburn, Kilmarnock, Scotland

ISBN - 13: 9781907731112

Copyright © 2010 by John Ritchie Ltd.
40 Beansburn, Kilmarnock, Scotland

www.ritchiechristianmedia.co.uk

Typeset by John Ritchie Ltd., Kilmarnock
Printed by Bell & Bain Ltd., Glasgow

Contents

"So shall my word be that goeth forth out of my mouth;
it shall not return unto me void,
but it shall accomplish that which I please,
and it shall prosper in the thing whereto I sent it.
For ye shall go out with joy,
and be led forth with peace."
(Isaiah 55.11-12)

Foreword

At a time when many people taking early retirement would be looking for an easier option, Robert Muir effectively took on a new and more demanding task. He set off to a Third World country to pursue a missionary calling along with Margaret Jarvis whom he had just married.

Much earlier in life, and at different times, both Margaret and Robert had come to know Jesus Christ as their personal Saviour and Lord in the west Fife mining towns of Lochgelly and Cowdenbeath, and as teenagers became members of the local church which meets in Union Hall. In 1966 Robert married Elizabeth Gibb and they spent 29 happy years together serving the Lord locally while Robert pursued a progressive career in nursing. He eventually became Deputy Director of Nurse Education at Fife College of Nursing and Midwifery. Integration of nurse education into the university sector made him redundant in 1995. That was also when the Lord called Elizabeth home to heaven after an illness bravely borne.

Margaret had trained in Fife as a nurse and midwife. In 1974 she heard God's call to missionary service abroad and was commended by her local church to work in central Africa. Her role as a nurse and midwife enabled her to bring the Gospel to many needy souls in several parts of Zambia and then Congo (at that time called Zaire). Her professional skills along with her fluency in the local languages, especially Bemba, gave her great acceptance with the people she sought to serve.

This book takes up their story from shortly after their marriage, and records some, not all, of their varied experiences in Congo and Zambia between 1997 and 2010. There have been highs and lows, joys and sorrows, but the story told here (with some considerable modesty) is a record of the faithfulness of the Lord to His servants as they ministered to others. It also demonstrates the fulfilment of a stewardship - of time and talents, of faithfulness to the teachings of Scripture, of finance and its accountability. The quality of their work has been recognised at home and abroad, the latter by their award in 2005 from the Zambian Government of M.C.F. (Member of Companion Order of Freedom 4th Division) for services to the community. Now living permanently in the UK, they continue to support the work in Mambilima and visit normally twice a year.

It is a pleasure to commend this book to a wide readership, as it has been a pleasure to have known the author for most of a lifetime, a pleasure recently enhanced by spending brief periods with them in the parts of Zambia described here. The book is written to inform, and to stimulate prayer for the progress of the work of God in Africa, and indeed all over the world. It is a great privilege and a duty for us all to be "helping together by prayer" (2 Cor 1.11).

Bert Cargill
St Monans
Scotland

Acknowledgements

Encouragement to write this book was made by many people saying to me that your experiences should be recorded for others to read. This is the outcome and I acknowledge with gratitude their promptings.

Grateful thanks to Bert Cargill for his capable work as Editor and for steering me on a straight course.

Thanks also to my niece Alison for guiding my computer skills to put this work together.

Thanks to my sister-in-law Florence for the detailed reading of the document.

Thanks to the publisher, John Ritchie Ltd., for producing the book in such a presentable format.

Lastly, my deepest thanks to my wife Margaret for all her loving encouragement and stimulation as we have recounted these incidents together as the work progressed.

Introduction

This short book has been written to put on record some of the many interesting experiences which Margaret and I had in the Lord's service in Congo and Zambia between 1997 and 2010.

Elizabeth my wife fulfilled her service for the Lord and He took her to her eternal home in 1995. The Lord brought Margaret and me together in 1996, and together we went to Luanza in Congo where Margaret had already been working.

Because of civil war in that country we had to flee into Zambia. We tried to get back into Congo but were able to be there for only short periods. When the situation became impossible we eventually settled in Mambilima in Zambia where Margaret had served as a nurse/midwife from 1974 – 80.

It was a real thrill for me to follow the steps of Dan Crawford from Scotland, and the many other pioneer missionaries who laboured long and hard in these areas. The situation had moved forward in the 70 years since Crawford died, yet in so many ways and fundamentally nothing had changed greatly. He was a man of vision to see people come to Jesus Christ and trust Him as their Lord and Saviour. But he also saw mankind, especially African man, in a wider view as body, soul and spirit, and as such must be catered for in a holistic way.

Here is how he saw the duties and work of missionaries one hundred years ago. In *Thinking Black* he wrote the following (p. 444-5):

"Here, then, is Africa's challenge to its Missionaries. Will they allow a whole continent to live like beasts in such hovels, millions of Negroes cribbed, cabined, and confined in dens of disease? No doubt it is our diurnal duty to preach that the soul of all improvement is the improvement of the soul. But God's equilateral triangle of body, soul, and spirit must never be ignored. Is not the body wholly *ensouled,* and is not the soul wholly *embodied?* Too often in Missionary literature the writer talks about these "humble abodes" of his black parishioners, whereas the real phrasing of the matter is that they are more *humbling* than humble. The more grandiose our Mission stations, the more striking and impossible the native huts. The louder, too, the call to gut out these clotted masses of tropical slums. Ignore this as Africa's burning question, and you commit the sad old folly of the Middle Ages - I mean when the Church built big cathedrals and men lived in hovels. Ever since those days back in Bihe when I lived with Mr. Negro *chez lui,* I have a plan simmering in my mind, a plan that involves one long street lined out for miles. The thing can be done and we Missionaries should do it. Oh yes, we are here for souls, but – I repeat it – the Negro soul is as wholly embodied as the Negro body is wholly ensouled. In other words, in Africa the only true fulfilling of our heavenly calling is the doing of earthly things in a heavenly manner."

Over the years in which we have been privileged to serve in Africa we have tried to follow such principles of care for body, soul and spirit. The following pages can testify to how the poor have been helped materially, physically and spiritually, how the Gospel has been preached, the Bible expounded to young and old, useful buildings and halls erected, a hospital and a school rebuilt and enlarged. It has all been done to the glory of God and the benefit of man.

Chapter by chapter unfolds a variety of our experiences. Some are so sad, others amusing, yet all are told in the awareness of the ability that God gave to adjust to every situation as it arose.

As you read may you enter somehow into our experiences. Encounter the various cultural differences along with us. Rejoice with us, and weep with us. Above all, seek to enjoy the hand of the Lord as you are taken with us along this journey in which we found fulfilled the words of Isaiah 55.12, "You shall go out with joy and be led forth with peace".

Robert Muir
Cowdenbeath
Scotland
August, 2010

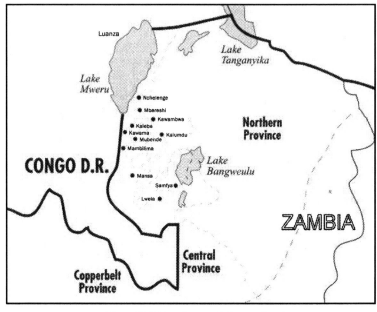

Map of NE Zambia and Congo Border

CHAPTER 1

First impressions – Luanza, 1995

The 300-mile flight from Lubumbashi to Luanza in the six-seater Mission Aviation Fellowship (MAF) plane, although rather bumpy, was fascinating. It was the rainy season, so everything spread out below was beautifully green. Small villages of grass-roofed houses with their slowly rising columns of smoke were dotted all along the route.

Soon the plane was over Lake Mweru. As we flew along the edge of the lake, the azure blue of the sky reflected in the water made it a most memorable sight. Little dugout canoes were scattered all over the surface and a *chombo* (ferry boat) plied its way down the lake. Then we saw it in the distance – Luanza, our destination!

Luanza is built on a plateau about one mile wide on the top of a cliff overlooking the lake. From the plateau paths lead to other villages higher up. The symmetry of the original village was easy to see from the air - built in squares with long wide streets lined with trees, most unusual for Africa. The founder of this village was Dan Crawford. His planning skills were very evident - it had all been built to his exact specification, a Christian village, known still as Crawford's village.

Landing safely we were greeted by what looked like the whole village and more. Cheering men, women and children in brightly coloured clothes, complete with goats and chickens, were everywhere. Ian and Marilyn Campbell greeted us and relieved us of our luggage. I was introduced to the elders of the church who prayed and gave thanks to God for a safe arrival in these "sheets of tin held together with rivets". A short trip took us to the Mission and into the house.

Dan Crawford's House at Luanza

Luanza is most beautiful in situation, built near the edge of this high cliff, looking over the lake to Zambia some 40 miles in the distance. Dan Crawford's original house dominated the Mission. From the outside it was pretty and quaint to look at, but now dilapidated and falling down, the thatched roof twice the height of the walls now infested with quite a variety of small livestock. An avenue of Ngashe Palm trees, planted by Crawford around ninety years ago, led the way to the church building. They yielded nuts giving oil in abundance every year. This reminded me of verses at the end of Psalm 92 where "the righteous shall flourish like the palm tree: ... they shall still bring forth fruit in old age; they shall be full of sap and green".

The church had prepared a welcome meal. Placed before me on a table was a metal basin containing a mountain of a greyish-white foodstuff. It was the African staple diet *nshima* made from cassava. Other bowls held chicken, beans and green leaves. Thanks was given to the Lord, and then our hands were washed by pouring on water from a jug over a basin. Being instructed on how to eat I reached out and took a handful of this stuff that looked to me like wallpaper paste. It came out like chewing gum, smelling foul and when it hit my stomach I knew it! I enjoyed it so much I took to liking it after all!

The hospital is in the centre of the mission compound. The midwifery department was very big and very busy. Margaret Jarvis and Shena McCall from Fife, Scotland, along with a number and a variety of nurses and midwives controlled the hospital. Tuberculosis was rife, and treatment prolonged. Many patients suffered from HIV/AIDS (Auto Immune Deficiency Syndrome.) This brought much grief as they just wasted away before one's eyes. Yet the age-old problem of malaria is still the largest single cause of death in Africa.

The out-patient department had many queuing up for treatment each day. One afternoon a family of nomads arrived at the hospital. Father, mother and children all appeared to be drunk, with slurred speech and staggering gait. They had eaten poisonous mushrooms by mistake. Now this commotion became a source of great merriment in the village. Many came to see this spectacle. They filled the windows of the room where the unfortunate patients sat on the floor, and could not be driven away. As for the cure – well, a dose of emetic was administered to each victim. Soon it worked and to the immense delight of all those gaping in through the windows the patients evacuated the contents of their stomachs into one strategically placed pail. I discovered that their curiosity and their sense of humour were different from mine! But the family disappeared into the night never to be seen again. The cure had worked.

Another night, the head nurse, a man of maturity named Mwamba, left his house to walk to the hospital. He was barefooted, did not have a light and was bitten by a snake. It was a Black Mamba, very poisonous - its bite usually causes death. We knew nothing until morning when we found poor Mwamba in hospital. His foot was the size of a football. The villagers had started to gather to wait for the funeral "wailing" to begin, such is the deadliness of such a bite. However, we prayed and sang a hymn to strengthen him in the Lord. He was given antibiotics by injection. Then the "Black Stone" was applied to the wound. This is a local remedy applied to bites and poisons. We are not sure how it works, but it certainly seems to! Soon the elders from the church arrived and more prayer was made and words of encouragement given. Mwamba lived and although his foot never returned to normal he continued to give great service to the hospital. God is good and rewards our trust in Him.

The hospital serves the community. One of its services is vaccinating the children in all the villages along the edge of the lake. This becomes a real day out. A 4-metre long planked boat with an outboard motor was used for the trip. This meant we all had to negotiate the hazards of the 100-metre high cliff to get down to the lake. Everything had to be carried. We protected ourselves well for a day in the open - hats, sun block and plenty water to drink. Shena McCall was in charge. Vedinique was captain of the boat.

The villagers heard us coming and welcomed us with great excitement. A mobile clinic was set up under the trees. Scales were hung from a branch, babies put into a harness and weighed swinging gently from the scales. All had their own jobs to do. Vaccinations were made both orally and by injection and records kept of each child. Then we had a short service - hymns were sung, a message from the Bible given and a prayer of thanksgiving offered. Goodbyes were said and it was off to the next village to repeat the procedure all over again. It became an exhausting but exhilarating and successful day.

At home in the UK many things are taken for granted for daily living, for example, a constant supply of clean water, electricity at the flick of a switch and a hot shower on demand. In this part of Zaire (now Democratic Republic of Congo) such things are a luxury not often available. Water came from two sources. One was a small stream which flowed from the hill above down to the lake, full in the rainy season but a mere trickle in the dry. The other source was a spring 2½ miles up the hill. This had been tapped and led by pipes into a large tank at the outskirts of the village. From there it was piped to various stand-pipes in the village and last of all to the mission houses. When a leak developed in the system the water supply failed - and it often did.

Water was heated in a Rhodesian Boiler. This consisted of a 200-litre drum built up so that a fire could be lit underneath it - a very effective way of getting hot water for washing, but no shower. Electricity was another matter. Solar panels charged some batteries which, with a converter, gave a good lighting system. The Mission also had a beautiful Petter diesel engine generator. The difficulty was getting fuel, as it had to be brought in drums from the capital Lubumbashi on near impassable roads. As a result the engine was run only from 6pm to 9pm each night. This was the time for the microwave to be used to do the cooking and baking. There was also a wood-burning stove with an oven. Here in the depths of Africa was a cooker made at the Carronshore works in Falkirk, Scotland. It was a great cooker - but difficult to control! – something to do with its country of origin?

The official language of the country is French, and the main local language is Bemba, one of the Bantu group of languages. My language is English with a broad Scottish accent! It was important that I grasp the greetings as quickly as possible so that at least I could communicate at a basic level. The headmaster of the local school who was also an elder in the church spoke very good English and acted as my interpreter. With his help I was able to do some preaching. It was a new experience, but soon I found a way to preach acceptably using short uncomplicated sentences.

One Lord's Day a baptismal service was announced to take place after the Gospel service. I was to preach that day. Choosing as the subject Acts chapter 8 and the conversion of an African from Ethiopia, I emphasised the meaning of baptism. Philip was answering the question of this African man, "What hinders me from being baptised?" Philip replied that if he believed, nothing should stop him. Both men went down into the water and Philip baptised the eunuch from Ethiopia. At this point in the service two young women in the congregation stood to their feet and cried out that they believed. These were the first conversions that I had experienced in Africa. The elders spoke to the two ladies at the end of the service, and to my surprise and delight they were baptised that day.

I did enjoy getting out into the village with literature, especially on a Sunday afternoon. Margaret would show the way. As we entered a compound they would call their neighbours. We settled down. I preached simply, Margaret put it into Bemba, and the Gospel was proclaimed. There was perfect liberty - the people so keen to listen to the Word of God.

Another day, Ian Campbell took a group of us to a church farther down the lake. I was asked to speak. As I sat on the platform a choir at my side rose to sing. A mother holding a fractious infant put it to her breast as she sang. Then she handed me the child and she went on singing. One had to learn to expect the unexpected!

Kabulemba is a village four miles up the hill from Luanza. They arranged a three-day conference for women and asked me to speak to them on Marriage and the Home. This meant a climb of over an hour up and down each day. Packing water, food, Bibles and books, off we went with the visiting party. The top of the hill gave such a panoramic view and time to get our breath back.

The little hall was on a plateau and much cooler. Soon it was packed with ladies sitting wherever they could. I could not move - my interpreter and I just stood still as we taught. There were two one-hour sessions in the morning and one in the afternoon followed by questions. It was rather tiring but I got used to it. I made an offer of a hymnbook to all who could memorize the books of the Bible. On day three I carried sixty books up the hill with great expectation of not carrying them back down. What a disappointment when less than ten took up the challenge and I did have to carry most of them back down!

The elders also arranged a five-day seminar on leadership in the church. This was a very profitable time as around twenty brothers gathered for the teaching of the Word of God over these days.

These were days of first impressions for me. It was great to be accepted and begin to feel part of the community. It was wonderful to see God blessing in His service and to know there were those who were trusting Jesus Christ as their Lord and Saviour. The surroundings were beautiful and the privations were no real hardship. The local food was certainly different and very plain but I was enjoying it. I felt that this was where I should be.

CHAPTER 2

Links with Dan Crawford

Luanza had many outstanding personalities. There were two old ladies of a great age in the church, having both known Dan Crawford. He had taught them English. Mary had never married, she chose to remain single so that she could devote herself to the service of the Lord - a very rare thing in African culture. She was a great visitor to the hospital and saw many won for the Lord. It was a wonderful experience to visit them both in Martha's home. We settled down and they sang a duet in English,

"As the deer pants for the water so my soul longs after Thee."

They sang beautifully, harmonizing together. What an enjoyable time of blessing that was!

Zeba was an elder, an old man who, as a boy, had worked for Dan Crawford. I got to love him. He suffered a stroke and was admitted to hospital. Although we had difficulty communicating with each other I visited him every day. Each time he said to me, "I'm still here!" then lifting his hand he would point his finger to heaven and say, "but I'm going there!"

His death was a triumph. As is the custom his body was dressed in his best clothes and seated in a chair outside his house in the village square. Many of the villagers gathered for the funeral. All morning the Word of God was preached interspersed with the choirs singing. During this time the sawing of wood and the hammering of nails could be heard - the coffin was being made. The missionary had the (doubtful) seat of honour sitting next to the body in the baking sun! Eventually around midday the body was taken into the house and placed into the coffin.

At 2pm the service began in the church building. It was packed full with the choir singing when yet another sound of singing was heard coming through the village. It was a choir of young people from Kabulemba at the top of the hill. They sang at full volume and without stopping marched right to the front of the hall and squeezed into seats still singing. Always expect the unexpected! A short message was given and a prayer of thanksgiving was offered, then the slow procession to the cemetery commenced.

The coffin was carried high by young men. Choirs sang in front and behind. They shuffled four or five steps forward and then two steps back. As they moved, great clouds of fine brown dust rose high into the air. But this truly was a triumphant march for one who had served his Lord well and who had now entered his rest.

On reaching the cemetery we gathered round the grave in its beautiful situation overlooking the lake. The coffin was lowered into the grave and a short committal message was given. Then the congregation sang in Bemba, *"Beulah Land."* I sang my words in English with a lump in my throat -

> *"Oh Beulah Land! sweet Beulah Land!*
> *As on thy highest mount I stand,*
> *I look away across the sea,*
> *Where mansions are prepared for me,*
> *And view the shining glory shore,*
> *My heaven, my home for evermore."*

What a goodbye to a much loved elder! The grave was filled in and we returned, rejoicing in the triumph of the crucified Saviour of sinners. Another had entered into eternal rest with Christ.

Considering this triumphant scene, I cannot help thinking of the great change that the Gospel has made in the lives of these dear African people. In their death God is honoured and the person is treated with great respect and dignity. I contrast this with 100 years ago, with a situation Dan Crawford described in an eyewitness account *(Back to the Long Grass*, p. 240-241).

"The air was filled with dust, tainted with the smell of heated African bodies and a sickly odour from the log fires. The evening breeze occasionally wafted the columns of smoke across the wild revellers, momentarily hiding them from view. By the lurid glow of the huge log fires, despite the almost fiendish appearance of the savages, I was deeply impressed with the vivid effect of the scene, with its action, and its striking contrasts. As my eyes grew more accustomed to the surroundings I observed many natives dancing at the edge of a deep hole which had been recently dug in the ground. Whilst leaning forward to obtain a clearer view, and conjecturing upon the object of the wild proceedings, I was startled by a mighty shout uttered from hundreds of hoarse throats. Turning, I saw several men forcing their way through the multitude in the direction of the dark abyss. A jingling sound of bells heralded a procession of dancing figures, whose forms stood forth in bold relief as they passed in front of the blazing fires. A space was cleared in front of the hole and in a few moments there bounded forth the great charm-doctor, painted and bedecked with leopard skins and rattling charms, outward tokens of the absolute ruler of the destinies of heathen African savages. This hideous-looking creature, with whitened eyelids and body smeared in fowls' brains and blood, commenced the Dance of Death. With sinuous movements of the body he pranced around the clear space, kicking up a perfect cloud of dust, and chanting a quaint savage song. Round and round, each time faster, whirled the uncanny figure. At length he stopped, bathed in perspiration, dusty and bedraggled, and seated himself at the edge of the hole.

Another hideous shout rent the air. Ten women, the former wives of the deceased chief, with hands and feet bound, were dragged forward and placed on the ground in front of the charm-doctor. Shortly afterwards a number of young men, formerly slaves of the chief, were also brought forward to the brink of the hole. Then amidst a scene of wild confusion the corpse of the great chief, now swathed in yards of cotton and grass cloth, was borne forward. Above the heads of the swaying crowd I caught the sight of dark bodies being hurled into the hole. I could just distinguish the agonising shrieks of women, the unfortunate wives who were being sacrificed. The body of the chief was next placed in the hole. The crowd surged, swayed and shouted even more vociferously than ever when a hundred hands commenced to heave earth into the living tomb of the chief's wives, who were buried alive. Hemmed in by the crowd I was unable to retire from the horrible scene. The hole was filled in and the natives danced upon the spot.

The first of the slaves were now brought forward. His head was fixed in a framework, suspended to an overhanging branch. A bright gleam of the executioner's knife, followed by a frantic yell from the multitude, denoted that the first of the numerous band of the late chief's slaves had been decapitated."

The message of the Gospel that we preach is one of life

and salvation, one of liberty and freedom in Christ Jesus. What a change it brings wherever it is received! Lifestyles are revolutionised, the dignity of women is upheld, slaves are set free. In place of dark despair and superstition there is the sure hope of eternal life and fullness of joy in the presence of the Saviour Himself.

* * * * * *

Some time later while we were in Scotland we received a telephone call from a Scottish lady who said she was Dan Crawford's granddaughter. Her name was Mairi Hedderwick. She was going to visit Tanzania and wanted to come to Luanza to visit the grave of her grandfather. We were not to worry about her arriving as she would get a boat over Lake Tanganyika and then get a lift in a lorry or whatever to Luanza. We assured her that this was impossible! However, one day she arrived with a friend into Zambia.

They hired a car to bring them to the border with Congo. Crossing the river on foot, they walked the 12 miles into Pweto. Reaching the *Boma* (Government Offices) they were interrogated roughly by customs and immigration officials. It must have been quite a sight as Don, Mairi's friend was dressed in his kilt and carrying a walking-stick. Their camera was confiscated as it was claimed they were photographing naked children at the lake edge. But Mairi had read of her grandfather having his photo taken paddling at Pweto, and she wanted a picture of herself doing the same. Some children were around when the photo was taken.

Next the walking-stick was examined. It was a souvenir they had bought in Tanzania. Upon investigation it was found to have a sword down the centre of the stick. "What's this?" the officials asked. Mairi answered by making a cross on the ground with the sword and scabbard and proceeded to do the "Highland Fling" dance while Don diddled the tune!

Eventually they were let go and they walked to Chamfubu where May Montgomery received them. The boat was sent to collect them. They reached Luanza exhausted.

At Luanza the church elders came quickly to see this very important person. This was her village, she was the owner! Mairi had never met her grandfather and had always been told he was a big ogre. He was too busy saving the people of Africa to care for his own child, the boy who became her father. Everyone she met was amazed to see the "child of Crawford" with their own eyes. It was very moving.

Zeba had longed to see her but had died a short time before. One old fellow who met her said, "He always spoke about his breeks," as he called his trousers! Knowing she was coming Zeba got the graveyard tidied up which was at the top of the hill, overlooking the village. Mairi climbed to see her grandfather's grave and also that of an uncle who died in childhood. The grave is covered with a large red sandstone slab. Harry Brown had erected this and engraved the memorial to the memory of Dan Crawford. This experience too was most emotional.

Mairi asked, "Why does everyone speak to me about my grandfather, but no one mentions my grandmother?" Then we went to visit Martha. Her little house was immaculate. Chairs were laid out and prepared for the guests. But she never expected Crawford's child to visit her! Beside Martha lay a pile of photographs. The first one Mairi lifted was a portrait of her grandmother, a beautiful lady sat in an elegant pose. Martha related how she stayed with Mrs Crawford when Dan died and comforted her in these days of grieving. Tears flowed as they hugged each other - what an emotional moment!

Margaret and I talked a lot with her about the principles by which Dan and ourselves lived, telling of how we trusted God for every aspect of our lives. We had only two nights together, and we trust that Mairi and Don left with a different view of her grandparents and their influence in Africa. On returning home Mairi wrote an article for a national newspaper entitled, "In search of the soul of my grandfather". It was a most interesting account of her visit to Luanza.

CHAPTER 3

Difficult days in Luanza

At Luanza the ground was most fertile. The fellow who looked after the garden had green fingers. Every day he would produce beautiful vegetables - tomatoes, onions, lettuce, cabbage, green beans, aubergines and peppers. Also in abundance were lemons, grapefruit and Mexican apples. From the lake below we were able to get fish, delicious breem. The Lord provided for our daily needs, adding a leg of goat and sometimes beef if a cow "broke a leg".

Mission Aviation Fellowship (MAF) flew in every two weeks and brought supplies from Lubumbashi. Most important to us was the mail they brought, keeping intact our link with the outside world. There was great excitement on these days as you looked for letters and outdated newspapers from home. We also had a short-wave radio which linked the missionaries in the Katanga Province. A call up was made twice or thrice daily to keep everyone in touch. When a medical emergency arose Dr Ray Williams gave excellent service and advice by this radio link.

As well as being involved in the hospital and working with women, Margaret and Shena had also classes for children and young people. Shena looked after the girls and it was good to hear them singing, and recite the Bible verses. Margaret had the boys' class. When I heard them singing they were rather off the tune. Then I learned that it was Margaret who had taught them the tunes!

Mungedi was one of these boys. His legs were so wasted that he could not walk and was carried everywhere. He trusted the Lord in those days at that class. Now 20 years later he turned up at Mambilima. It was sad to see him carried on the back of a bicycle, but he was going on with the Lord and enjoying fellowship in a church in his village. Another of these lads joined the army. He was just a boy. Sitting on our doorstep he gave a demonstration of stripping down and cleaning his AK47. It was like playing with a toy. Such were the boy recruits for the army.

A children's meeting in the garden was announced. Using visual aids and with Margaret as an interpreter I tried to teach them. It was an interesting exercise since about 200 had come. At the end of the meeting two barrow-loads of lemons were ready to give to them. We tried to control the distribution but what a scramble it was! - more a rugby scrum! What children will do just to get a lemon or two!

Christmas day was like any other day. The children came gleefully from the village chanting, *"Noeli, Noeli."* They had high expectations, but we had so little to give - a lemon and a few sweets were our gifts, all they would receive that day. They went to the Christmas Day service, sang the carols, re-enacted the Christmas story, listened to the message and went home. Their meal was the same as it usually was – *nshima*, beans and green leaves. I compared it with Christmas back home and the vast amounts of money lavished on the children there. Then I wondered - who were the happier ones?

* * * * * *

With the Military Coup and a change of regime, things became difficult. We had to flee the country a number of times and then we got back in again for a short time. The first time was soon after I arrived. Radio contact said, "Time to get out!" Ian and Marilyn Campbell, Shena, Margaret and I quickly piled into the vehicle and headed north to Pweto. Very little was taken for the journey. Meeting up with May Montgomery and Jean-Luc and Rita Hainaut we spent the night at Chamfubu. Leaving early next morning we headed for the *Boma* (Government Offices) to get our passports stamped for exit. The plan was to get to the Zambian border, ford the river and cross into Zambia. The officials were reluctant to let us go, but after much prayer things did move. Two senior army officers said they would take us to the border. This was the Lord's provision.

Time and again we were stopped by people wanting to take our vehicles. The army commanders kept us on the move. Eventually we reached a real road block. We could go no farther. May Montgomery was quickly out of the vehicle and disappeared into the village. As we sat there a soldier came past with flip-flops on his feet and a serious looking grenade in his hand. He put that hand in through the window and made as if to drop the grenade. We sighed with relief and praised the Lord as he withdrew his hand. Then May returned - she had found a way through the village, and off we went again.

On reaching the shore of the lake we came to the border post. It was only a grass-roofed shelter. Again the bargaining started to get our passports stamped to allow us to leave the country. But nothing would move – that is until the Lord intervened. Out of a cloudless blue sky He sent a violent rain storm, real torrential rain coming horizontally right into this grass shack of a border post. The officials quickly stamped the passports and off we went! We hadn't gone more than 100 metres when the storm turned and went down the lake. This was not the first time our Lord had shown His authority using a storm!

Now the river had to be forded. We were prepared for trouble, taking ropes and planks with us in case we were stuck. The Landrover went first. The Lord guided the way and the Toyota followed and then we were safely out on the other side. What rejoicing as we were free! Zambian fishermen at the lakeside shouted and sang for joy as we reached the shore. "You are free! You are free!" they cried.

Another time Margaret and I were travelling from Zambia to Lubumbashi. The going was good and we were within sight of the city. Then, rounding a corner we were confronted by a soldier with a gun pointed at us and forcing us off the road. It was an ambush. Along with others he robbed us, and fired off his gun at Margaret's ear. We cried out loudly to the Lord. Suddenly they stopped, took some bread and marched off. Giving thanks to the Lord we collected our goods which had been scattered everywhere, got on board the vehicle again and continued with our journey.

The next village was nearby. They had heard the gunshots and were waiting for us. A union official kindly came with us on the rest of the journey and took us to the Governor's Residence. The place was full of large expensive settees into which we sank down - so thankful for the peace and quiet again.

The governor was called away so we were allowed to go. Eventually we arrived at Rest-a-While to a warm welcome from the missionaries. After a quick resume of our story the dear lady said, "Come and I will get you a cup of tea." Margaret replied, "If you had been my father he would have given me something stronger!"

Having composed ourselves and dressed a bit better we went to keep an appointment with the Chief of Police. His office was a complete contrast to the governor's place round the corner. In the ceiling there was a light bulb holder but no bulb. He called for chairs but the old attendant could not find enough for five of us. After much palaver we settled down, all except Walter Raymond who had to balance on a stool with one leg missing. Now the serious job of taking a statement commenced. But it was getting really dark. Each time we said a sentence the police chief had to leave his seat and go across to the window to write it down. This continued until it became impossible and we left. All that night we laughed and laughed till the tears came too, release at last from that eventful day's tensions.

On another occasion MAF came to fly us from Luanza to Pweto. Since there was much trouble around we had arranged a sign with Jean-Luc at Pweto if it would be safe to land. The pilot that day was Jim, an American who was extra meticulous in his preparations. As we flew over Pweto we were looking for the safe sign. We could see Jean-Luc standing talking, but the sign being given said 'Unsafe'. As we circled, it dawned on Jean-Luc what was happening and he altered his position to signal 'Safe'. Touching down, however, we were met by soldiers running out of the undergrowth surrounding the plane with all guns pointing at us. We asked if it was safe to come out. "Perfectly safe!" said Jean-Luc, "they are using this as an exercise!" Pilot Jim never left the plane! He quickly taxied to the end of the runway, and without fuss or the usual checks he was in the air. He said, "Bye-bye and I won't be back for you!"

The official sent to Luanza by the Government was an awkward fellow. He was always looking for ways to extract fines from the hospital for his own pocket. He continually visited to check our drugs and stock. If he found anything that was "best before" he said it was out of date and accused the staff of poisoning the patients. He accused of using cotton wool that was out of date! We had a supply of ex-British Army high protein biscuits. They were 40 years old, had been in sealed boxes and were very nutritious. The village chief loved them as they kept him healthy. Well, our official found them and forbade us to give these away. The chief was devastated. So we left them lying out and if the chief wanted them he had to help himself. No questions were asked about what happened.

The two senior men at the hospital in Luanza were accused of various misdemeanours by this man and sent to Pweto with a letter to the chief official describing the charges. Off they went. Margaret and I followed them by boat to support them. What a journey that was! Thunder and lightning came down on the lake. We were soaked and took shelter in a village. Eventually we reached Pweto. No transport was available to take us to the mission 2½ miles up the hill. We started to walk. The rivers were swollen and we just had to wade through. Reaching the mission, May Montgomery welcomed us. Lanfuti, the man who helped around the house, asked why we had come. "Our staff have been summoned to see the chief because of some accusations," we said. "Who?" he said, "the Chief? That is my son David, I will call him immediately." David came and within a few minutes the matter was settled.

In the morning we were on our way back with a letter summoning the Luanza official to see his boss. The ways of God are past finding out!

The Bible says to commit our ways to the Lord, and He will direct our paths. Experiencing His care and protection in so many ways we have often bowed before Him and given thanks. It became impossible for us to get back to Luanza and so we waited in Zambia till we were guided to the place where God would have us to serve Him.

CHAPTER 4

From Pillar to Post

The number of missionaries fleeing from Congo into Zambia put great strain on the available accommodation. Mark and Shirley Davies offered us their house at Samfya for two weeks as they were on a journey. This was our first refuge. The mission is in a beautiful situation overlooking Lake Bangweulu. We explored the area around the village, as we slowly recovered from our experiences.

Down in the harbour we found, lying at the bottom of the lake, the wreck of the *Galilee*. This boat had been used by Mr and Mrs Coleman and Mr and Mrs Houghton to take the Gospel to the fishing villages along the lake edge and on to the peoples of the swamps. They used to live on the boat for weeks at a time. It was so sad to see it now dead and buried in the lake.

There are two Christian Missions in Many Lands (CMML) churches in the village. One is Bemba speaking the other English. The Bemba one was large and very lively. Many, on hearing the good news, had placed their faith in Jesus Christ as their Lord and Saviour. The English-speaking church was much smaller. Among the announcements that day was a call for all to help with a big clean up of the building. The dear brother said, "Now! See all the web-cobs in this place; we need a big clean-up. So all come with your hoes on Saturday!" The congregation burst out laughing and we smiled at the new use for hoes!

During these days we were learning to be patient and wait the Lord's time. Soon we were on the move. Accommodation was offered us in a flat at Luanshya. It was upstairs above some shops and across the street from a night club. So it was rather noisy each night - as the band was very loud and as alcohol took effect many a fight broke out, making it difficult to sleep. The bed was a water bed. It wasn't filled properly and the heater didn't work! Every night we wrapped ourselves in blankets and swished and swashed all night long - not the most enjoyable of experiences!

In the town there was an antiques dealer who sold everything! We went in for a look round. Hanging from the ceiling was a wooden sign. There was just one word on it, "awaanbileyerheidacomefigovan". I asked the owner for the meaning of this unusual word. He said quite proudly, "My name is in it." His name was "Figov". There it was almost at the end of this unpronounceable word! However, for the benefit of those who cannot read the Scots tongue, being translated into English it reads "away and boil your head, I come from Govan". Govan is a well known district of Glasgow. How it got there we cannot fathom!

At this time we received an invitation from Ray and Terry Barham to live with them in Mansa. They had a guestroom which we could have till we settled. This was most interesting as their house was the one Jim and Margaret Kennedy had lived in several years before, and Margaret is my full cousin. In the Zambian culture she was my sister!

Ray offered to try and teach me the Bemba language. He is a real expert in Bemba and an excellent teacher. But he was doubtful of my ability as he had never known anyone over 50 years old learning it. I worked hard at it for three months, but I was nearer 60 than 50 at this point. At the end of the three months it was obvious I would never manage to preach in Bemba as in English. So I decided it would be better for me to settle for speaking through an interpreter. This I adjusted to very quickly.

During this time Mr Thomas Kabwesha was hired daily to help with the studies. He was an interesting fellow, a retired school teacher whose subject was music, unusual for Zambia. An elder in Mansa mission church he devoted his time to visiting the CMML churches in the district. He taught the choirs how to write their songs and sing them. Each day he also taught the Bible to these dear folks.

My lessons were held outside under a mango tree. Afternoon temperatures become very high in Zambia. Many a day as Thomas was teaching me his voice would tail off and he would fall fast asleep. There was great embarrassment when he wakened! He could interpret my Scottish accent very well and together we visited many churches in the Mansa district.

Visiting a village 10 miles outside Mansa we found an old church elder had died early that morning. I was invited to take part in the funeral service to be held outside his house in the village. The corpse was sitting there, upright in a chair, clothed in his best suit. Many had gathered around under the blazing midday sun with very little shelter or shade. The choirs sang and I gave a message from the Scriptures. During all this time the arms and legs of the body were being exercised to keep them from becoming stiff and powder was being liberally applied to keep down the smell. More choirs sang, we all sang, and more speaking. I asked Thomas the reason for the long wait. "The coffin," he whispered!

Then into the compound came a young man with a bicycle. He was panting and puffing and bathed in perspiration. Strapped to the carrier of the bicycle was a beautiful coffin. He had been all the way to Mansa to buy it!

It was taken into the house and the corpse was lifted gently and placed into it. The sound of hammering was heard as the lid was fastened on. We were now ready for the burial. Someone came over to me and asked me to use my vehicle as the hearse. I couldn't refuse! The coffin was loaded and we were off on the slow walk to the cemetery where at last the dear brother's body was interred.

The church always gathered for prayer on a Saturday evening at the hall on the mission. Margaret and I always attended when we were in town. On going to the hall one evening we found the door locked. The only other person to arrive was one very old lady. We waited and waited but no one else came. As we stood reverently, I prayed and thanked the Lord for His goodness and then asked a blessing. Still standing, as if to attention we sang the customary closing benediction "*Kuli Lesa tuletota*" which is

> "*Praise God from whom all blessings flow,*
> *Praise Him all creatures here below,*
> *Praise Him above you heavenly host,*
> *Praise Father, Son and Holy Ghost.*"

God says, "Call on Me and I will answer." Numbers do not matter. Jesus said, "Where two or three are gathered together in My Name, I am there" - whether in a building or under the open heavens. We felt His presence that Saturday evening!

We enjoyed our stay in Mansa. Ray and Terry and their family cared for us. We enjoyed the fellowship of Ruth Gray and her daughter Hope. The Christians in all the churches made us welcome and we got to know the folks of the town but now the time came for us to move forward.

The folks at Musenga always made us very welcome when we visited them. Philip and Valerie Grove had a "Granny Flat" attached to their house which they now put at our disposal and we lived here for a number of weeks. It was good to see the working of the printing press and to be able do a little work around the place. It was also good to be involved in teaching from the Bible in the English-speaking church.

These were formative days allowing us to see many aspects of the work of God in that part of Zambia. God was teaching us to wait on Him. When He directed us to go and settle in Mambilima we were ready to obey. After arriving and settling in to the work it became very evident why the Lord wanted us in that place.

CHAPTER 5

By the Lakeside

I well remember the first time I arrived at Kashikishi. It was in 1997, the day we had escaped from Congo by crossing the river. Eight very weary, exhausted travellers arrived at Mweru Water Board Guest House at midnight. The night watchman was at his post, fast asleep on a couch. Rousing him from depths of slumber we enquired about rooms. "We need four rooms please." He said, "I have two." Then it was three, and eventually four! They were provided – "so long as we did not need to eat," he said. Marilyn Campbell produced pot noodles and we boiled water on a picnic stove and we ate with a hunger-induced relish.

We found a very active church here with many others in the surrounding area. The elders wanted Margaret and me to settle here and give help in this community, but we did not feel it was right to do this for a variety of reasons. There was already a body of capable elders and deacons who were forward looking. However we did become involved in the work.

Jonas Katontoka was a most wise and capable teacher. He had come from Luanza and had been educated at the mission school there. He had an insight into missionaries and their ways. One day he said, "You are *eyefilyako* (not so bad, a little all right) - if you could just get on with each other it would be okay." He went on to give the reasons for his statement. It is not often you get such a frank expression of what the locals think of you!

45

Puta is Jonas' son and a hard working evangelist. He reaches out to the nomadic people of the forest. In one tribe he preached the Word and saw sixty people trusting the Lord for salvation. Staying with them he taught them and many were baptised. They soon met together to break bread and remember the Lord. Recently this was repeated in a village near Kashikishi and another church commenced.

Evangelists who reach into rural Zambia

In another nearby village where the Gospel was preached, a witch doctor trusted the Lord and was baptised. He took his place with the believers but he had great problems. This converted witch doctor had been a very powerful fellow in the village being revered and held in awe by most. The people were afraid of him and now that he was converted the believers did not know how to handle the situation. The dear man was having trouble being accepted – remember Paul after his conversion? Brother Jonas was the man used to help to make the necessary adjustments for the good of all.

The church at Kashikishi had a great desire to have a bookshop and a school where the Word of God could be taught. We felt it was right for us to be involved in this. At this time we had received a gift for some project, and from it the Clifton Christian Centre arose. The church building was on a large site and it was decided to expand and build here. We had no problem with planning permission.

The church rose to the challenge of making bricks. The best clay was found down by the lakeside at the other end of the village. The bricks were moulded and allowed to bake in the sun. These bricks had to be carried up the cliff to the roadside for onward transportation to the site at the hall. What a sight it was to see young and old, men and women all being involved. Bricks were carried on heads, in barrows and in boxes. Now these bricks are big, nearer the size of concrete blocks. Jonas took his cycle. To see this elder, an old man, strap two bricks to his carrier and push it up the hill was to see leadership in action. The people had a will to work.

At the building site a large kiln was made and filled with wood. It was set alight and the bricks were fired hard. So the work commenced and soon a building of three rooms, an office and a bookshop were complete. These rooms were a classroom and sleeping accommodation for males and females. A *nsaka* (an open area with a grass roof) was made outside for cooking.

The bookshop had an enthusiastic start. Many Bibles and books were sold at subsidised prices. A young man, the son of Chansa was in charge. As well as working in the shop all week, on a Sunday he would pack two boxes and strap them onto his cycle and go and visit other churches. Many were reached in this way.

It was a joy to see the Bible school commence. Ba Chansa led this forward. He was a capable teacher of the Word of God and also head teacher of a primary school. He had great ability to confront others who came with false doctrines. However after some years he contracted diabetes which was very unstable. It was difficult to get a constant supply of insulin and as a result in a short time he passed into the presence of the Lord.

Leonard Ngosa is another able teacher of the Word. He had come over to Zambia from Congo and was a good French speaker as well as being fluent in Bemba. He had a remarkable gift for languages and taught himself English. His preaching is enthusiastic and dynamic, being used over a wide area for teaching. He took forward the Bible school.

On commencing the Bible school the believers were asked to bring food to help feed the students; the food was brought in abundance. For the first and only time in my experience I heard an elder ask the congregation to stop giving. It has been said that the spiritual state of a church can be assessed by its giving.

I did find teaching these students a great challenge. An outline of the Bible was given. When dealing with Exodus, I was to give some teaching on the structure of the tabernacle. One day we could not get an interpreter. I asked Margaret to help. Well it was most interesting to say the least as she struggled to put over the concepts of posts and boards, of stays and pins and everything else. A lesson was learned quickly – don't allow your husband to ask you to do something like this! More success came with the project we introduced - to make a scale model of the tabernacle. It was wonderful to see their ingenuity – what materials they used to make it. Certainly no fine gold or silver was found. After one Sunday morning service it was erected outside and the students gave their explanations to the congregation.

As the years progressed another set of classrooms was added. Then the Clifton High School was commenced. At present they have ninety students in Grades 10, 11 and 12. As part of their studies, Scripture is taught and many of the students are saved and in the church fellowship. When Dr Bert Cargill visited with us in 2004 he spoke to over a 100 students on the subject of Creation versus Evolution. That was a most interesting and lively morning with many questions asked and answered.

One is always aware of the power of witchcraft. A young man in the village who had been involved in witchcraft trusted the Lord. Making a public confession before the church he then proceeded to burn the objects he had used. It is most important that such persons renounce clearly what they practised. Another witch doctor gave his life to the Lord. He made his public confession at the conference to all gathered. Then he set on fire all his paraphernalia. As he did this there were shrieks and cries from many in the company as they expected demons to jump out of the fire. The power of Satan is real, but our God is all powerful.

One day a young man was brought over to the village from Congo by a soldier. He had abducted the man and was trying to sell him. The poor fellow would then be killed and his heart taken out. It would then be put under the doorstep of a shop to bring success in business. The plot was foiled when a Christian businessman got to know about it. Those involved were arrested and eventually the young man was taken back to Congo. Evil is all around - only the power of God can bring true release.

The Government Offices are at Nchelenge and there is a nice church here. They set out to build a new hall, which became a real credit to them. Isaac and Dorothy Kabwesha always made us welcome there. They had a large extended family with many children who had been orphaned. This is so usual in Zambia because of the HIV/AIDS situation. They have a real love for the work of God.

One day while Isaac was interpreting for me, a man in the congregation came down the aisle and threw himself prostrate on his face in front of us. He lay motionless. I was taken aback as we waited in silence. Isaac motioned to me to wait. After what seemed an eternity another elder came and encouraged him to stand up. God was at work convicting him of a wrong in his life. An elder came and took him away to give counsel. One must always expect the unexpected!

At Kashikishi we found accommodation in different places. Mweru Water Board Guest House was the one we used most often. It was on the edge of the beautiful lake, with steps leading down to the sandy shore. There we could relax a little after a day's teaching. The bedrooms were passable but the dining facilities were another story. We had many a laugh. We asked for a menu.

"Do you have fish," we ask.

"No," was the answer, "we only have 'flying fish'."

In the Bemba language there is not an R. So it turned out they had only 'frying fish'!

"Can we have chips?"

"Yes," was the reply "if you bring the potatoes!"

We learned to take our supplies with us. One morning a Zambian businessman from the city and his son arrived for breakfast. With bated breath we waited for this new encounter. When the 'waiter' came he asked if he could have 'a continental breakfast'?

"You mean cornflakes etc? Yes – No. We do not have cornflakes nor milk!"

"What can we have then," he asked.

"You can have fish and chips."

"What!" the man said, "at this time of the morning. No thank you!" We shared our cornflakes and milk. We laughed and laughed.

There is a big fish market here down at the lake side. One must be prepared to haggle for a good price. There are different prices, one for Zambians and another for *basungu* (white people). We could never get the best prices! When we were buying supplies for the school we would get one of the believers to do the buying for us.

Kashikishi has a warm place in our hearts. We poured a lot of time and energy into the work there. The church had a real vision for the work of the Lord, and gave themselves wholeheartedly to it. The elders lead from the front and the flock follows.

CHAPTER 6

Refugee Work

Returning from a village trip one day in 1999 it was a strange sight to see a steady stream of people walking along the roadside. They were mostly women and children. All were poorly clad and carried very few belongings. They looked weary and exhausted, dragging their feet. We asked who they were and where are they going?

We found out that they were refugees from the war in Congo. They had fled their homeland and entered Zambia at the Kashiba entry point. Zambia was kindly welcoming such refugees. They were making their way to a UNHCR (United Nations High Commission for Refugees) transit camp about 18 miles farther along the road. They had been walking for weeks, many with bare feet.

We felt that we should get involved and try to give some help. We visited the camp two or three times a week which put a strain on our work load but it was of the Lord. Their stories were pathetic. "Why so many women and children and so few men?" we asked. They had either "disappeared" or been taken prisoners. Many had buried children who had died on the journey; they were so weak. The numbers arriving varied - some days few, other days many. Twice a week the UNHCR sent down a covered lorry which took them from the transit camp 150 miles farther on to the permanent camp at Kala.

Nothing was being done to provide food for them in the

transit camp. The local health officer was a Christian and wanted to help, but the Government had no supplies of food or medicines so we moved in to help. From the local market we bought maize meal, green leaves, cooking oil and charcoal. Locally we also obtained *chesense* (small fish, like whitebait). Oh the delight on the children's faces when they saw the *chesense!* They danced and whooped for joy chanting, "*Chesense, Chesense!*" It was the first they had had for weeks!

Their general health was in a poor condition. So we also provided some medicines. One family we took to the hospital at Mambilima to be treated for severe malnutrition. From supplies we had received from the UK we were able to provide clothing and blankets. The churches in Mambilima also became involved. Out of their poverty they gave - a shirt here, a dress there, until a sizeable collection was made. A group of believers were taken to the camp to hand over the gifts. This was followed by a short service and prayer was made for them there. How grateful these people were!

One day at the camp we saw literature lying all over the ground. "Where did all this come from?" we asked. "People came with this literature and wanted to preach to us," they replied, "but they brought nothing to relieve our hunger!" It was from the Watchtower Press. James in his writing reminds us that faith without works is dead!

Many of these Congolese folks were believers. We followed up the work and visited the main camp at Kala. It was on a beautiful site high on the plateau which had been given by the Zambian government. Under the control of the UNHCR it was well organized and efficiently run. Each family was given a piece of ground, sheets of plastic and some wooden poles. They were instructed where and how to build their own shelters. The camp was laid out in squares, each being identified by designated lettering for identification. There were around 28,000 residents at Kala.

The facilities were really very good. A clean water supply was collected from stand pipes which had been plumbed into strategic places all over the camp. Toilet and ablution blocks had been built. There was a health post and also a small hospital. A number of schools were built, both primary and secondary. Teaching of English had been included into the curriculum. It was a most impressive set up.

But supplying food for such large numbers of people usually has problems. We noticed that the supply tents appeared to be full. On investigation we found that they were filled with sacks upon sacks of green peas – all very nutritious and full of protein but they were disliked, indeed loathed! The result? - grumbling in the camp! Remember the children of Israel with the manna? They too loathed the food! That was angels' food, and the Israelites could do many different things with it. But there is a limit to what you can do with green peas! We found the discontent had spread to the believers as well.

At this time a container of food had arrived from Scotland and Mambilima had received its share. A truck was loaded with food and clothing and driven to the camp. Like the Lord's disciples we thought, "What is this among so many?" The administration at the camp was under the control of a very distinguished Indian Commander. He had the answer. The tins of nutritious food were given to the hospital in the camp. The weak ones were provided with a more varied diet to encourage them to eat. The small amount of food went a long way!

There were many Christians in the camp. We found a large functioning church of around 500 believers. Given a piece of ground, they had worked hard to build a beautiful hall from tree saplings intertwined with reeds. From their allowance of food the Lord received His portion. They traded their allowance with the people around the camp, exchanging food for planks of wood. They then made beautiful benches for the meeting place. From their poverty they gave what they could and the Lord blessed them.

One day we took a group of our brothers from Mambilima to visit the church in the camp. Gatherings were held morning and afternoon - the hall was packed. I am always amazed at how many can be seated on a single bench! The children sat all over the platform. There was no room to move! A number of us taught the Word of God, and it was a real time of encouragement for everyone. We had taken a good supply of French, Bemba and English Bibles, also French and Swahili books and Bemba hymnbooks which were left with the elders for the believers to use.

The believers insisted that they provide the lunch for us. It was a marvel to us to see the spread! They had *nshima* and chicken, rice and fish, with green leaves. Their generosity and self denial humbled us and caused us to give thanks to our God.

A number of the believers had come from Chamfubu in Congo. One of them, Kamfwa, was a good teacher of the Word. Lanfuty and his wife were there. Others had worked at the hospital with May Montomery. Many were industrious and started up small businesses, some of them trading in beans and fish. Some even came as far as Mambilima to sell their produce to us.

But many will never leave the camp. They enjoy the safety and security of Zambia. Some have found suitable partners and have married, and now have no desire to return to their homeland. Reminds us of the contentment many Jews had in Babylon in Old Testament times!

God is blessing His work in the camp. There is now a variety of preaching points all around it. People are trusting the Lord

- being saved, baptised, and added to the church. We praise God for how we were able to be involved in this development in its early stages.

CHAPTER 7

Kawama and Links with Bermuda

Kawama is a village on the Luapula river approx 40 miles north of Mambilima. There has been a CMML Mission here since 1929 when Mr and Mrs George Lammond commenced a work there. Many names of former missionaries have been associated with Kawama - Ken and Dora Kruse, Mr and Mrs Wilson Beattie, Misses Mitchell, Oddy and Reid. It was known as a malaria black spot and very unhealthy. For this reason there was a high turnover of personnel.

The old mission house is still standing, now a derelict two-storey building in a rather dangerous condition. I could never understand why, with so much land around, missionaries built two-storey houses! When asked they said it was to be kept safe from lions and other wild animals! All the bedrooms were upstairs. Now there are no wild animals except snakes.

A new single storey house has been built. Some believers from Bermuda sent a gift for this purpose. Sims Mwansa, who is a hard-working farmer and energetic evangelist and his wife now occupy this house. Visiting churches over a wide area, he gives much pastoral support and help – a real man of encouragement.

He had a great desire that the Scriptures should be taught systematically. So three days were set aside each month for teaching; they loved to call it a Bible school. Around twenty brothers and sisters would often come and eagerly give themselves to serious study. These were profitable times as most parts of the Old and New Testaments were studied.

In time a Bible bookshop was added to the site and it became a focal point in the district. To keep it afloat financially they sold a few groceries and a fridge was added for cold drinks. Later another building was added for the students to meet and study the Word of God. Before that, many a time we had gathered under a tree because the sun could be so fierce. It is great to see how the interest had been sustained over the years.

Each year at harvest time, Sims would prepare a large sack of maize and give it to the Lord to be used in His service. It was the firstfruit of his crop. He said that it was his "tithe" - he was the only farmer that I knew to do this!

Over the years Sims encouraged a great many young men, but he was greatly saddened when a number let him down. With Kawama strategically situated on the main road he was often inundated with visitors, many expecting to be lodged overnight. His dear wife often had to produce a meal from nothing!

Mrs Sims was a character in her own right. She loved to wear the brightest of clothes, always with a matching head-dress. She even managed high-heeled shoes – where they came from I know not! When we were on a journey and arrived at her house she was always going in our direction! She needed transport of course. How she learned that we were coming was impossible to know – but it happened every time.

The churches wished to get a boat because they wanted to evangelise the fishing villages along the edge of the river. Sims organised a contract with a local boat builder. As is the custom, part payment is made on commencement.

Weeks later we enquired about the boat. We learned that it was completed, the builder had sold it and kept the money! We tried again. Who received the contract to build this time? The same local boat builder! This time we were successful and the boat arrived. We were able to purchase a second-hand outboard motor. The first time they tried it, it fell off the boat and into the water. They were successful the next time. With everything now secure and the tank full of petrol they were off on a preaching tour.

Some time later we asked them, "Where is the boat?" "It has gone to the islands to help the brothers with preaching and fishing," they said. Well it is being used for the Lord and the community. You learn to shrug your shoulders and see it from their point of view.

Lukwesa is a market village near Kawama. A young church met in a disused Customs shed as they prepared to build a meeting hall of their own. One Sunday morning we met with them for the Breaking of Bread. The table was covered with a white cloth and the emblems were in place. As the believers arrived they brought their offerings and laid them at the foot of the table. What an offering! - maize, cassava, pumpkins, groundnuts and bundles of green leaves. One old lady hobbled in and placed an egg on the table. So much was given. They had little money but gave freely of their substance! They sold the goods afterwards for money.

In a very short time the bricks were burnt and foundations laid for the new meeting place. They worked together, receiving some help from neighbouring churches. Soon a beautiful hall was erected. They worked and the Lord worked with them. How good it is when brethren dwell together and work together in unity.

The village of Chipunka was 10 miles north of Kawama. They had an enthusiastic group of young people here. They arranged seminars for Sunday School teachers on a monthly basis for about six months. These were happy days as the teachers came together from the surrounding churches. The Word of God was taught, also communication skills, the making and use of chalk boards and visual aids. The ability to learn through play was taught, teaching the teachers to play with the children and use it to get to know them better. There was a great spirit of oneness in these times.

In this area the choirs asked for a seminar for them to be taught the Bible. They meet to write their own songs and sing them in harmony, also fulfilling a social function for the younger and older Christians to meet together. It is good to see them as part of a local church.

Being involved in this district was a blessing to us, and we trust we were a blessing to them also. Sims Mwansa has recently had a stroke and although recovered he is now more limited in his abilities. But his desire for the well-being of the church is still as great as ever.

CHAPTER 8

Island Hopper

The long Luapula river flowing north with Congo on one side and Zambia on the other eventually widens and enters Lake Mweru. There are six sizeable islands here on which a number of churches have been planted. Responding to a request we decided to visit them. "How do we get there?" we asked. "By boat," was the reply. This would be a new experience.

Sims Mwansa arranged for a group of elders from these island churches to come across for us at Kashikishi. When they arrived we found seven strong "paddlers" in a 4-metre planked boat, and we were also seven, plus our luggage for the week! Leaving the Landrover in the safe keeping of the Kashikishi Fishing Company we prepared to sail. The company manager was anxious for our safety. He came and inspected the boat and the paddlers, then, assuring himself all was well, he let us go. So off we went into the unknown, thirteen men and one lady plus luggage!

It was a beautiful day, calm and bright. After an hour of steady rhythmic paddling we reached the first island. But sitting on a hard plank of wood does soon become uncomfortable – at least for the passengers! Passing it by we continued to the next island. Here the church was expecting us and already many believers were waiting. What a wonderful welcome we received. After we landed they escorted us to a beautiful little house they had built.

It was made from reeds and grass, very bright and cool. The bedroom had a grass-filled mattress, the living area had a table and two chairs. What comfort! We lay down in peace. After a short rest and some refreshment it was time to meet the church. It was such a privilege to bring the Word of God to these dear people. Later sitting round the fire we discussed many topics with them. Later still they brought us some lovely hot water for washing, and off we got to bed. They had gone to so much trouble to give us such a welcome.

Next morning we left early as it was to be a long day. Making sure we were protected from the fierce sun with sun-cream applied and hats on, it was out under a cloudless sky on to a calm lake. On and on we went in that fine boat. The discussion and banter among the crew in the boat was stimulating. I took a short spell of paddling. It was short, but a welcome change of position, for our posteriors were sore with sitting!

Eventually we reached the mouth of the river. Over a hundred years before, Dan Crawford had come this way to get to Mambilima. As we sailed down the Congolese bank we passed many little villages, picturesque with their thatched roofs, spirals of smoke rising into the still, hot air as they prepared their food. Around noon we reached our first stop, a fishing village on the Zambian side of the river. Climbing out of the boat with rather stiff legs we eventually managed to scramble up the bank onto the shore.

After a short rest they provided our lunch, given out of their poverty - fish and *nshima*, it was delicious. Then the church gathered to hear the Word. Psalm 2 was the reading: "Why do the nations rage and the people imagine a vain thing?" "Yet I have set My king on My holy hill of Zion." God has all things under His control everywhere. It was a great time of encouragement for us all on that island too.

Then it was into the boat and off again! A bit farther downstream we turned into a narrow channel and kept going until we reached a large lagoon. It was idyllic - the water was so still, reflecting the azure blue of the cloudless sky. The large water lilies were majestic in their various colours and hues. The only sound was the drip of water from the paddles and the occasional cry of a bird. It was so beautiful and peaceful. In special times and places like these you stop and worship, for God's creation is so utterly majestic. "The whole earth declares the glory of the Lord."

At the far end of the lagoon was the next island, our destination. Leaving the boat we walked for about an hour this time. Our goods and chattels were carried on heads or shoulders, primitive style. Nearly there, a lady was heard to exclaim, "What is the world coming to! The white people have arrived!" This was the first ever visit of a white person to their island. However, by now it was late so after eating we went to bed in a little village house, very basic but comfortable. Next morning the church came together to be encouraged by the Word of the Lord.

Taking our leave of them we walked on to the next village where we lodged for the next three nights. The local evangelist and his wife were our hosts. Their house was on a little plot of ground with a well in the garden. It was great to sit round the fire under the trees in the cool of the evening discussing the Scriptures. Leonard Mukuku, our head teacher, was our interpreter and he enjoyed this too. The little girl of the family called all her friends to come and help her "stare at the white people". You get used to the children sitting beside you and running their fingers up your arm. They need to know if a white skin feels the same as their own! All quite harmless!

The next day was the Lord's Day and we walked about two hours to gather with the believers. It was an unforgettable experience to break bread with these dear people. The village chief was in this fellowship. He sat among the others around the emblems on the table. "I am not the chief when we gather – I am a brother in Christ," he said. These village chiefs are men of great power in their own sphere, but how lovely to see him sitting under the authority of the Spirit and the Word!

Gifts were given to us en route as a thank you. Here the gift was a large pig! It had to come with us to the boat then in the boat. It grunted, squealed - and stank! - the whole way. First there was a two-hour walk to get to the boat. Margaret had the privilege of a ride on the carrier of a bicycle, not the most comfortable of seats!

At the shore, the chief insisted that I wait for the luxury of a boat with an engine arriving, while Margaret went off with the paddlers in their one! It was a least an hour before my boat came. By this time the paddled boat had almost arrived at the other side. However we caught up with each other in a narrow, shallow channel. With so little water the crew had to get out and push the last stretch!

The expedition was almost over. The fish lorry took us back to Kashikishi to collect the Landrover. The goods and the pig were duly transferred. Eventually we reached Mambilima. The pig, now know as "Robert's Pig" was fed and fattened. Its condition was regularly noted in the minutes of the Board meetings. What next? Eventually it was killed and eaten!

It is so worthwhile to be able to make such a trip to help Christians who live in such isolation. They live in extreme poverty, eking out an existence from the lake and the land. Their love for the Lord Jesus was clear to see. Out of every kindred, tribe and nation God is calling a people for Himself. The Lord Jesus said, "I will build My church." Clearly He is doing that all over the world.

Zambian Lake "Ferry Boats"

CHAPTER 9

In the Highlands

Kawambwa is a town in the highlands on the plateau to the east. It is fresh and cool here with a clean water supply. Ntumbatushi Falls are en route, a most beautiful site, luscious and green. The water is clear and cool, a great place to relax and safe for swimming.

From here the road to Kawambwa climbs up the escarpment. It is very steep and twisted giving panoramic views at the summit. One day a lorry loaded with maize and forty high school boys on top lost control. The brakes had failed and the vehicle rolled over at speed and hit a large rock. Nearly all the boys were killed, one of whom was the only son of a Bible teacher. He was identified by a letter of commendation from his pocket. This was a national tragedy - so many bright young men called into eternity. How important it is to be ready for such events when we are young! A day of national mourning was held and a state funeral given.

There are several residential schools in Kawambwa for both boys and girls. They have their Scripture Union groups and the Word of God is taught. Also there are a number of churches in the district, the central one having the hospital nearby. When visiting I was surprised to see so many planks of wood in the hall. They were on the floor, beneath the seats, and on the roof trusses. "Why all the wood?" I asked. "It's for the *bochoses,*" they replied. The wood was for making coffins! They were responsible for burying any CMML church member who died in the hospital. This custom was putting an impossible strain on this church.

John Chanda and his wife were in the church. He was a senior teacher and she a community nurse in the town. They were both hard working and had a heart for the work of the Lord. Both were involved in getting Bibles, books and literature into the hands of the people. This trustworthy pair did a lot for the spiritual welfare of the believers.

About 18 miles distant is a large tea estate owned by an Indian family. They employ many people and it was an interesting experience being invited to tea with them. They were very supportive of the work of believers in the local church. While there we lodged with Emmanuel Musonda and his wife. He is the accountant for the estate.

A tour of the tea processing plant was very informative. The tea leaves were hand picked from the bushes, then brought into the factory for processing. Placed on large trays they went into an oven to be dried. They used eucalyptus wood from a renewable forest to fire this oven, thus giving the tea its distinctive flavour. The leaves are then graded. The larger the leaves the better the quality - the poorest goes to make teabags!

Arriving at Emmanuel's home one day we found it surrounded by a mob. The whole village appeared to be there. They had stones in their hands. Entering the house we asked what was happening. Emmanuel had been accused of killing the next door neighbour's child with witchcraft. If any of his family left the house they would have been stoned. Indeed a brother-in-law tried this and was attacked. The 'prince of the power of the air' is powerful. The child had actually died from a bad attack of malaria.

What do you do in such a situation? This had gone on for days. We read the Scriptures, prayed, sang hymns and encouraged the family to stand fast in the Lord. Sadly almost all of their brothers in the Lord forsook them. I was reminded of our Lord in the days of His trial – all forsook Him and fled, leaving Him alone. In such occasions the village chief wants to send in the witch doctor to divine and find out if the family are responsible. They will look for something in the house with which to accuse them. By sleight of hand they will plant an object and on finding it will accuse the family or an individual of having an evil spirit.

The believer must be strong to resist this. The believer's body is the temple of the Holy Spirit and no evil spirit can reside in him. Emmanuel and his wife stood firm and came through the experience much stronger in their God.

It was here I first encountered a highly nutritious drink called *munkoya*. It is made from millet. Drink it immediately and it is good for you, but leave it for a day and it ferments and becomes potent in its alcohol content. We cautioned the believers about drinking this, as it was commonly used as an alcoholic drink. We must resist every appearance of evil!

We attended a conference in the next village. A brother who had succumbed to alcohol was challenged by the Spirit of God. He threw himself on the grass before the congregation crying to God for mercy. It is not easy to be released from the grip of alcohol.

A young lady here had been badly burnt. A wire rope

used for drying clothes had been tied from a tree to her house. Lightning struck the tree, came along the rope and set the house on fire. It shattered a large mirror on the way. The dear lady had a miraculous escape!

Mushota was a village about seven miles at the other end of the *dambo* (marsh land). Patrick and his wife and family lived here. He worked for the Government's agricultural department. This lovely family always made us most welcome. In preparation for our visit the dear lady washed the foam cushions from the chairs. They had been out drying all week. Being offered a nice comfortable chair I was glad to sit down. But before long I felt wet underneath! It is most embarrassing to walk with a large wet patch on one's seat!

Justin and his wife lived nearby. They had been married for three years but as yet had no family. Both sets of parents were putting them under great pressure to leave each other and get another partner. It is most important to have a family. This creates a big temptation for Christian couples. They asked us to pray for them that they would be kept faithful to the Lord and to each other. We did this and gave them good counsel. God was gracious and in the fullness of time a little baby boy was born.

In a small church some distance away we were lodged with an old widower. At breakfast time that morning he produced an old-fashioned mincer, then he proceeded to give us minced boiled sweet potatoes to start the day. Out of his poverty he gave freely! He was badly crippled, walking with great difficulty using crutches. He was usually taken to the gatherings sitting on the back of a bicycle which was a great struggle for him, but he loved the Lord and did not want to be absent.

It was a real joy to visit these small rural churches. How they appreciated the Word of God! We were able to give Bibles and books to help strengthen them in their faith. Here, as elsewhere there is a great need of Bible teaching. Perhaps modern technology needs to be explored more to help to establish these Christians in their faith.

CHAPTER 10

The Domain of a Chieftainess

Kashiba is only six miles from Mambilima and is the nearest crossing point into the Democratic Republic of Congo. There is an Immigration and Customs Post here. It is always useful to keep in touch with the Immigration Officers. They are powerful Government officials and can be very helpful.

There are three churches here all in close proximity to each other. Good fellowship has been enjoyed with them and much help given, both spiritual help and practical care. Chief Kashiba is a very nice Christian and is in fellowship in the church, a distinguished looking man with beautiful bushy black hair, quite unusual in appearance. A good chief can have such an influence on the community. This chief is hard working and introduces many projects to help his people. Such individuals can have a difficult time as they stand for God in a heathen culture!

Heading in an easterly direction the road takes you to the "mountain". This road really cannot be classified as a road but rather a track up the hill, strewn with rocks and boulders, almost impassable except for a 4-wheel drive vehicle. Many vehicles have become unstuck trying to climb or have overturned coming down. The Landrover was just right on this terrain. Putting her into the lowest crawling gear she would pick her way up and down the hill - it was always better to be well loaded coming down!

Reaching the top of the hill the road levelled out and the

surface was better. Mukabi was the first village. Most of the men here are woodmen, planting and cutting trees. Here we could purchase the most beautiful *mukwa* (mahogany), much of which was bought for building work at the hospital and school. A few believers lived here but generally it was a godless place.

In the next village there was an active church. Krispen and his family lived here. Many groundnuts and maize were exchanged for Bibles. Krispen gave us a real scare one day. Coming to a conference he contracted cholera. By the time we knew about this he was in the clinic at Kashiba and at death's door. We thought we had lost him, but God was gracious. With a lot of intravenous fluids and antibiotics, good food, tender loving care and prayer he pulled through. How quickly illness can strike. We are so grateful to the Lord for His protection when hundreds gather at conference times.

The road continues until we reach Mwenda. It is very cold on the plateau but beautiful and clear. Invited to spend a Lord's Day here we left early on the two-hour journey. Arriving at 9am no one was to be found. Eventually a brother arrived. "They will be slow to gather today," he said. "It's very cold." How we could have enjoyed a hot cup of tea! It was 11am before the folks started to come. By this time the sun was out at full strength. We remembered the Lord and the Gospel was preached.

The chief here is a lady, a very formidable person who keeps her people under control. It was quite an experience to have an audience with her in her palace. Her daughter, Beatrice, is a lovely believer in church fellowship in the capital, Lusaka. Lady chief is a good farmer and grows very high quality beans. We negotiated to buy some for the school but she drives a hard bargain!

At Mwenda we found a young man from the USA. He was

with International Peace Corps. Such young men and women give a year or so of their life to work in some rural community. They live in the most basic conditions, existing on as little as possible, travelling on bicycle or on foot. At Mwenda this fellow was developing fish farms for the community with a fair degree of success. In conversation with him he showed a great interest in spiritual matters. Later he came to a conference and bought a Bible. We trust he went on to read it and give his life to the Lord.

The road from here is a graded dirt road which becomes much wider. For miles it was like travelling over an old-fashioned washing board – full of ruts. The speed must be kept up so you ride on the top of the ruts, but by the time you reach your destination your bones are well shaken!

Kalundu was the next stop. This was the birthplace of Mr Ray Barham who is now at Mansa. It was a rather desolate place with white sand and black rocks and very little grass. The glare of the sun reflecting from the sand was quite blinding. Mr Barham's parents' house was still in the village. It was to be our lodging for the night. But there was no glass in the windows and the floor was covered in a fine black dust – like the coal dust we knew in our youth! With some difficulty the blow-up mattress was inflated, then down we lay on the floor and went to sleep. During the night we rolled off the said mattress a few times. Next morning it was blackened whites that got up to start the day - not an endearing experience!

Mr and Mrs Budge had lived here at one time. She was a character who was loved by the villagers in the area. She went everywhere on a bicycle. To get to her house she had to cross a stream. Lifting her bike she walked sure-footedly over a plank of wood. When she died the villagers chose a burial site at a crossroads so that she would be remembered as they passed by!

There is an active church here at Kalundu. They reach out with the Gospel and teach the Word faithfully. The time spent was very profitable. Then we received a request to visit Katilye. "It is nearby," they said.

Retracing our steps for a short distance we turned south into a forest track. "How far?" I asked again. "Oh it's about 15 miles," they said, pointing with the chin down the track. The road was full of holes filled with water, the depth of which was unknown. A fallen tree blocked the path. It had to be circumvented – how grateful we were to be in a 4-wheel drive vehicle, and onward we went. Eventually after 50 miles the village was reached! - "nearby" in Zambian terms?

Katilye was in a beautiful location right at the top end of Lake Benguela. This lake is very high above sea level. The Luapula River starts here and flows north via Lake Mweru then west and south merging with the mighty River Congo and after about 3,000 miles reaches the sea at the Atlantic Ocean. The area was flat with luscious green grass all around this bright blue lake. The elders came and the church was called together. As our visit was unexpected a smaller than usual group gathered to hear the Scriptures taught. Another date and time was agreed for a longer visit.

The promised date arrived and with three elders with us we made the journey. Negotiating the "mountain", passing Mwenda, and then down the 50 miles of track, at last we arrived. But they had forgotten we were coming! "No problem," they said, "we will arrange."

"Where do we sleep?" I asked. "The school room is available," they said. But there were no windows or curtains, just an opening! "Where can the three men sleep?" we asked next. There was a small room at the back of the class they could use. But there was no privacy for Margaret and me so we decided to sleep in the Landrover. The school room was at the edge of a large football field with the nearest toilet facilities at a house at the other end of the field. The washing facilities were in a grass shelter there also.

Putting some screening around the windows of the Landrover we lay down on a single mattress on the floor. There was little movement that night. Then it started to rain - a proper downpour! Closing all the windows we tried again to sleep. Amazingly, like the psalmist found, the Lord gave sleep to our eyelids!

In the morning we were wakened at 5am by what seemed like a hundred little faces staring from the veranda of the school room. They wanted to welcome us to the new morning! I felt the bed cover, it was soaking wet. Looking up at the Landrover roof it was covered in condensation and dripping like a shower. But soon the sun came out and the clothes were drying. The same performance took place the next night!

The children were so excitable and also uncontrollable! It was not every day that white people came to their village. However the Sunday School teacher could cope and control them with the help of a cane!

The meetings were a real blessing as the Word was taught over the weekend. Our physical discomfort was well compensated by their interest in the teaching. And soon again we were retracing our steps all the way back and down into the valley.

CHAPTER 11

Idyllic Lagoon

Musonda is a village 24 miles south of Mambilima. There is a hydro-electric plant here, fed from a reservoir high in the hills at Chisheta. The water flows down into a wide, idyllic lagoon at Musonda, then through a culvert to feed the power station.

Daniel is an engineering manager at the power station and an elder in the church at Musonda. We have enjoyed much happy fellowship with him and his wife and family. They are a big-hearted couple, taking into their family children of relatives that have been orphaned. They care for them as their own and educate them. This is not always the case when orphaned children join a family. They can be treated as second class citizens.

Another interesting couple here are Mr and Mrs Mbita. They are quite old but look after grandchildren of a young age. They too have fulfilled their duty and looked after them as their own. Such situations are replicated time and again as so many parents die from the scourge of HIV/ AIDS. It is always a wonder to see how they manage to feed and educate all the children.

At Musonda the church went to work and built a new hall. It was a struggle but they gave themselves to the work and completed it with some help and encouragement from others. An unusual geological feature of this area has resulted in a natural supply of beautiful coloured marble-like flat stones. A batch of these was gifted to the believers and used to line the lower half of the inside walls of the hall to give such a lovely finish. They converted their old hall into a place to care for elderly saints who did not have anyone to look after them.

The village lies like an amphitheatre around the lagoon. The market place is very poor with little on offer but they have the most delicious tasting bananas! They do not look anything special but the taste is something else! You have to "taste and see ..." - reminds us that God does not look at the outward appearance but on the heart!

The head teacher from the village took ill and eventually died at Mambilima hospital. No transport was available so I was asked to take the body and the relatives back to Musonda – I agreed! What else could I do? The body was carefully laid on the floor of the Landrover. Then the relatives piled in. How many? I know not! Insisting that there be no wailing on the journey we set off. As I reached the top of the hill and started to descend into the amphitheatre something amazing happened. It was as if a message was flashed round the whole village. Wailing burst out in the vehicle. From all over the place, villagers streamed down the hills.

How did they know I was coming with a corpse? I cannot tell. The wailing was horrendous and got louder as we reached the house of mourning. Without Christ there is no hope! Also, there is another reason - you need to wail or else you may be accused of causing the death by witchcraft. Such is their great fear of the spirits.

On arriving in the yard things moved swiftly. The house was emptied of what furniture they had. The body was taken inside. The wailing continued. Fires were lit. The people were preparing for a long night at the funeral. The choirs come to sing, and it goes on all night. It gets very cold. Resistance is lowered. The mosquitoes are fierce. Many catch cold, flu and malaria. Because of singing all night they lose their voice and are ill for days! But this is their custom and tradition!

The village before Musonda is an interesting little place. This was one of the first places we tried exchanging produce for supplying Bibles and hymnbooks. At the appointed time they were waiting with their groundnuts and maize for our arrival. The price of exchange was agreed - so many "tins" or "gallons" for a Bible or hymnbook. The believers had made a great effort to gather together enough for the exchange. We had to do some creative accounting so that they could have their "treasured possession" but it was a worthwhile experience!

At this village they had the most dilapidated Gospel Hall by the roadside. Directly opposite on the other side of the road the Jehovah's Witnesses had built a beautiful Kingdom Hall. This was the jolt they needed to do something about their rather uninviting meeting place. With some encouragement and help a lovely new hall was built right in the heart of the village.

A conference was held in the village, down by the river under the trees. This is the river that flows from Musonda and feeds into the Luapula. At the conference they arranged a baptismal service. Baptisms are performed in the river but there is always the risk of crocodiles! So the brothers stand in the water in a semi-circle while the baptisms take place within it. On completion, everyone comes out from the river together as one. The croc will always go for a straggler! – a spiritual lesson here?

About seven miles after Musonda on the road to Mansa a track leads off into the bush. There are three churches down this road, the farthest being about eight miles distant. The church in this village had sent representatives to us requesting a visit. The ladies wanted help to start a sewing group.

With a date and time arranged, we went on the journey. The track became narrower and rough. We had no idea how far we had to go - it took ages to arrive. When at last we did arrive the whole church was waiting for us. They were expecting some Bible teaching as well as the requested help for the sewing class.

An elder here, a little fellow with a short twisted arm, said he would do the interpretation. He announced that, before I taught from the Scriptures, I would say some words. So warm greetings from Scotland were given, and I outlined some of our work as missionaries in the Luapula. His interpretation of this was that "Robert had come to bring them anything they wanted! All they needed to do was ask and it would be given!" Margaret, horrified, sitting in the audience raised her hand and said, "We are getting two different messages." He was giving his own message, the one he wanted them to hear! The dear brother suddenly realized that Margaret could hear and understand Bemba! But did he get embarrassed? Never for a moment!

The teaching was given and the believers listened well. But all the time I was conscious of the smell of alcohol from the interpreter. When I finished I called Margaret and told her. She confirmed my suspicions and challenged the dear old fellow. He flatly denied any problem of drink, but he did keep moving away from us.

Alcohol always presents a big temptation and can bring problems to some believers in the bush churches. There is so little ability among them to handle such situations when they arise. Also the ability to expound the Scriptures is very limited. Many of these believers cannot read and do not even have a Bible to refer to. Consequently meeting at conferences is a vital part of Christian life and vital for feeding God's people.

Returning from this village on another occasion a woman ran from a house and flagged us down. She said her daughter was in labour but could not deliver. Putting the girl into the vehicle we drove to the next village where there was a clinic. The nurse on duty was not to be found – "gone to her gardens" they said. Margaret got the girl onto a couch and using a poly bag as a glove examined her.

All was well and she was well on the way to delivering the baby. An urgent message was sent to bring the nurse, then we were on our way. Leaving her I said, "If it's a boy his name is Robert, if a girl – it's Margaret." The next time we passed that way the young mother ran to meet us. "Come and see little Robert!" she said. Unfortunately there is no R sound in Bemba so it was an interesting Zambian variation of a Scottish name!

On the other side of this river that feeds the Luapula is another track road. The way across the river is by pontoon. Negotiating slowly down the steep bank you get the vehicle into position on the deck and the wheels are chocked. Passengers and crew then pull together on the wire ropes and slowly the other bank is reached and we proceed ashore.

When intending to cross one day, it was unsafe to use the pontoon because the river was so full and flowing so fast, that a planked boat was being used instead. Parking the vehicle where we thought it would be safe we reluctantly agreed to get into this boat. Gingerly we took our place, sat down and prayerfully committed ourselves to the current. Sure enough, the oarsman skilfully landed us on the other side. Then we walked this time, thankfully, to our destination!

There were nine churches down this road, one in each village. Sikila was the name of the first. This is where old Jakob lived. He was a character who shuffled along on worn-out shoes. He was a widower who lived on his own but had a great heart for the Lord and His people. When he came to Mambilima for a meeting he always arrived early after a journey of at least two hours calling at our house as he knew breakfast would be supplied!

At the service here one Lord's Day a show of Bibles was requested. Only three brothers had a Bible but none of the women had one. Margaret spoke to the ladies to find the reason for this. After leaving school they married, had children, and just worked in the home and in their fields. They had no reading material and so had lost any reading skills they once had. Speaking with the elders I discovered two or three were teachers who undertook to give lessons to the ladies. Simple reading books were supplied, and purchase of Bibles was encouraged. There was a big improvement on the next visit!

The believers were keen to evangelise and went visiting other villages. In one village where they preached the Word they discovered there was a group of around thirty believers. As they preached another thirty trusted the Lord. After some teaching was given, most were baptised. Soon they were meeting to break bread to remember the Lord. Every week two elders from nearby churches went in rotation to give help and establish the new believers. It is wonderful to see the work spreading like this and churches being planted. There are now ten churches on this road!

All over the district there is a great need to teach the

Scriptures systematically. From the Word of God believers need to learn the fundamentals of the faith. Those who are young in the faith are otherwise more open than ever to the attacks of Satan! We ought to pray even more for their protection.

CHAPTER 12

Mambilima Rural Hospital

There has been medical work at Mambilima since the 1920s. This followed the return of people to the area after an evacuation because of sleeping sickness. From very humble beginnings this work has gradually developed, so that now a wide range of health care and spiritual care is offered.

Officially the Government classes the hospital as a Rural Health Centre. Although upgrading to hospital status has been promised repeatedly, as yet this has not been granted. At present it is being used as the referral hospital for the surrounding area.

The original buildings were made from mud bricks covered with mud plaster. This type of structure is easily invaded by white ants which destroy the walls and the timbers, causing many problems. Roof beams have to be renewed regularly as they are eaten away by ants.

There was a desperate need to build an outpatient department. Patients were being examined outside in a grass *nsaka,* with no privacy for such consultations. Through a gift from a sister in Scotland, the Murray Outpatient Department was built. This included a waiting room, two consulting/treatment rooms, a records room and a dispensary. So patients can now wait in comfort until they are seen in appropriate privacy.

More of the old buildings were demolished and this freed

up space to build two medical wards for women. The provision of these came about because each week an old sister in Scotland had conscientiously put aside some money in a polythene bag. When it was full she handed it over to be sent for the work at Mambilima. The sum was substantial and with it the McQueen Medical Wards were built.

The original building itself had to be demolished before it fell down. This left an oblong area which was designated for building an operating theatre. The small size of the area rather limited what could be achieved. It was to be a community project, but unfortunately because of inability to work together nothing more than the foundation ever materialized. After waiting for a long time for unfulfilled promises it was decided to move forward on this project. A straightforward plan was drawn up and passed by the authorities. Cement blocks were made and the work soon began. Now there is a modern operating theatre which functions well within its limitations.

When it was first reported that a doctor would be coming to work at the hospital there was great excitement. The then administrator said "We are getting a doctor, we better hurry and build a mortuary!" He did not appreciate our laughter!

Over the years other wards have been demolished and replaced. Two wards for men and a new laboratory have been built. The hospital is now a counselling, testing and treatment centre for HIV/AIDS. The pharmacy has been brought up to a high standard. There are also two rooms for the accountant and a community officer, and next door is a teaching room/boardroom.

A dental suite was added and this is a great blessing to the community. The latest building is a high dependency unit for malnourished children, a great many of whom are still found in the district. This four-bedded ward has extra heating. Next door is a kitchen to be used for extra feeding and teaching.

In the grounds of the mission a ten-roomed building for housing the relatives of patients has been built, and over the years several staff houses also. We look back and see the many ways and the many people God has used to provide resources. There is now a great need to replace the maternity unit. We are confident that in the Lord's time this will be done!

Mambilima Rural Hospital

Within the boundary wall extensive landscaping has been done, with orange and lemon trees planted, and *ngashe* palm trees have begun to produce nuts. These fruits are a beneficial supplement to the diet of patients and staff.

There is always great emphasis put on the spiritual side of the care given. Each morning there is a service held in the hospital, relayed over the tannoy so that all the patients can hear the good news of the Gospel. Personal visitation is encouraged, literature is given to the patients and many prayers are made. Many women and some men have come to know the Lord during their stay in the hospital.

It is sad to have to report that over the years stealing and corruption has been a problem. It was obvious that a proper wall-fence round the hospital was necessary. Villagers were walking through the grounds and helping themselves to what they saw and no one challenged them. Mattresses mysteriously disappeared off the beds and "no one saw anything"! On one occasion 32,000 penicillin tablets went missing from the hospital. Antibiotics and other drugs could not be accounted for. Someone said, "Go to Dickson's store and you can get any antibiotic you want." I went and found that this was true. Pinned up on a shelf were plastic bags with many kinds of antibiotics. I bought a treatment. It was sold to me in a plastic bag marked GRZ (Government of Zambia). Where did they come from? Who can tell what was the truth?

The police stopped the hospital minibus going out of the village one night. A senior member of staff was driving. It was full of all manner of goods. The driver gave the officer a reason for the transportation, and the police did not question the matter any further. Mattresses and whatever else had gone! We praise God that such thieving now appears to be under control.

It is many years since the last missionary doctor was at Mambilima. For a short time we had a Voluntary Services Overseas doctor with us. Dr Sue loved her work and was great with her patients. She was a believer who did not normally gather with CMML and she let us know it! But we worked well with each other.

One evening returning from a village trip we were met by local villagers who told us to hurry. Dr Sue was very sick. We found her with a severe attack of malaria. It was the first she had experienced and she thought she was dying. Intramuscular quinine was prescribed. She objected strongly - she did not want a big needle for the injection! "Listen, doctor, you are now the patient!" and the appropriate big needle was used to good effect. "Margaret," she said, "have you room in your freezer for my body?" She did not want to be buried in Zambia!!

Sue did not like or believe in homeopathic medicine. But because of the persistent violent vomiting she was offered some medicine to help. "I'll take anything," she said, and after an hour on the medicine the sickness ceased. Amazed, she said, "It actually works!" Unfortunately she had to return home before her contract was completed as her mother was very ill.

More recently John Moyo was a clinical officer at the hospital. He had great potential and was a good clinician. He was encouraged to apply for a licentiate course, was accepted and completed four years of study. He then returned to give great service to the patients at Mambilima. Those who complete this course have difficulty being accepted to upgrade to full doctor status, and this can cause such individuals to be disgruntled. But John was reading his Bible and as he moves to other service we follow him with our prayers!

Doctor Zulu is a Zambian who has now joined the staff. He is very well liked by patients and staff and he also has a keen interest in the Bible. It is difficult to attract doctors and nurses to work in a rural situation. Over the years good housing with water and electricity has been built and this has helped to attract staff. The possibility of having television by satellite is a pull for others.

Over many years the hospital has been a focal point in the village. It has been used for the blessing of the community and for bringing glory to God.

CHAPTER 13

Mambilima Special School

In rural Zambia, attitudes to handicapped children vary. In general they are not accepted in the community and they are often shunned by many villagers. Without intervention they would probably spend aimless lives hidden away somewhere.

Many questions are asked as to their disability such as, "Why are they handicapped?" "Is it because of witchcraft?" A child who had a leg amputated was asked the reason for this. "Oh, it was because of a frog!" he answered There is still a lot of fear and superstition around.

The school work in Mambilima district commenced in the early 1900s. When Flora Lammond died in 1906 there were 25 churches of believers and also three schools in the district. Ethel Woolnough commenced a school for girls in 1926 and was responsible for its functioning. Charles Stokes was also involved with school work, among other things. In 1936 he married Ruth Pickering and both of them were involved in this type of work.

Meryl and Betty Shepherd came to Mambilima in 1944 and 1946 respectively. They were responsible for many schools in the district. Betty started the school at Mambilima Mission itself as a school for blind children.

In 1964 the Zambian Government took over the responsibility of running village schools. At this time the number of blind children at Mambilima School was decreasing. So it was that eventually in 1975 children who were physically handicapped were introduced to the school, and the Government became responsible for the blind children.

Over the years since then this special school, dedicated to the needs of physically handicapped children, has expanded. Through it all the love of God is being shown in a very practical way as disadvantaged children are being cared for and are receiving a good education. As a result the Lord Jesus is being given a place in the hearts of many of these young people. It is quite a unique facility in Zambia. Its motto is "Disability is not Inability".

A significant year was 2004 when the dilapidated original school building was replaced by brand new larger premises built over several months by a capable team from UK-based Brass Tacks (British Assemblies Tactical Support.) Assisted by a sizeable local workforce, the new classroom block soon took shape, built round a large assembly area and complete with proper access facilities for wheelchairs.

At the same time as building the new school, the Brass Tacks team doubled the size of the dining room. The school was then expanding to take Grades 8 and 9 so this was of great benefit. The dining facilities are basic but appropriate to the needs of the school - simple, nutritious food is supplied three times a day, mostly *nshima* made from maize meal, with beans and green leaves.

In 2010 a high school was opened with one class in Grade 10, anticipating that grades 11 and 12 will be added in the next two years. The expansion of the facilities to provide this High School for physically handicapped children was an important step. One of the reasons for this is the great pressure for children to get into higher education, and normal school facilities are not always suitable for children with handicaps. So after negotiations with the Government authorities, permission was granted for the high school to begin.

Once again more accommodation was required. Plans were drawn for a block of three classrooms with office and storage facilities. In due course a grant was received to help with the project. A beautiful building is now in place with full wheelchair access to all rooms, and a delight in which to teach.

Another hostel for senior boys was required next. A strong building made from cement blocks was lying empty nearby - a piggery which had not fulfilled its original purpose. This has been renovated and converted, and now the senior boys have taken up residence there. It is to be hoped that the boys don't turn it back into a pigsty!

A completely new building was provided for the senior girls' hostel, built with kiln-fired bricks and cement. It has eight rooms, with two girls sharing each room. There is also a large study/sitting room, toilets and showers – altogether a great facility for the girls.

Some characters

One very clever boy who gained a high pass mark in Grade 9 was granted a place at a prestigious school. He came from that area and could live with his brother nearby. The head teacher there refused to take him into the school. "Take him away," he said, "we don't want blind children here." "Sir," we said, "he is not blind - he has a walking difficulty but can cope with it." "He is not coming to my school," he said, "he has been at a school for handicapped children." After much persuasion on our part he was forced to reconsider and the boy was reluctantly accepted and is doing well.

Beauty was another very bright young girl who was selected for an up-market girls' high school. Again the female head teacher refused to take her. The education authorities said the girl must be accepted but the Head said, "No!" After much debate it was agreed that if a special toilet and washroom was built for her she could come. Mambilima staff dug a toilet and built a washroom for her there and so she took her place. There is such a fear and dread of witchcraft!

Some Schoolboys

The children are all different. Many are little characters with great personality. How they manage to overcome their disabilities is amazing. Like any other children they have good and bad days.

Nathan was one such character. He had only half of one arm and was a likeable rascal. One day he was seen digging a big hole in the ground. "Nathan, what are you doing?" we asked. "I am on punishment," he said. His teacher being asked what he had done, replied, "I can't tell you - it is far too bad to mention!"

It transpired that after dark one night he had climbed out of the hostel and had taken a cob of corn from a plant. He then borrowed a *babula* (charcoal burner) and roasted the corn and enjoyed his "forbidden fruit". Well, we had to be very serious and respond suitably. But we had a good chuckle later as we thought of the incident!

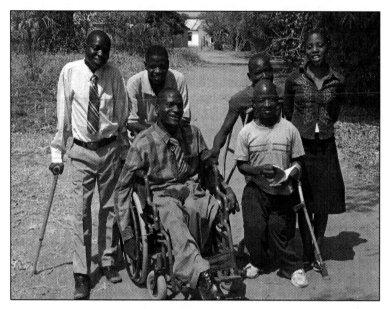

Some more older ones

Sunsetti was a child who lived out in the bush with a severely handicapped grandfather. The old man doted on the child and would not part with him. Sunsetti was very small for his age and had very wide bowed legs. After a lot of persuading, his grandfather allowed him to come in to the school. The improvement in his health was immediate. He was bright eyed and keen and his legs straightened naturally. It is wonderful to see what good care and good food can accomplish.

James came from a very poor family which lives in a distant village. He had a severe scoliosis of his spine and was a sickly child. Because of the disability he was unable to do much lifting or hoeing. He was a likeable lad who often came around the house where we lived. He applied himself to his studies and went on to high school. At present he is waiting for Grade 12 results. He wants to go and study accountancy in further education.

All the children are given good food regularly each day as part of their physical care. Also a Zambian orthopaedic surgeon has taken a great interest in many of them, and has performed many corrective surgical operations on their limbs. The result is that many of them have been able to do without their crutches and now walk and run around normally.

Their spiritual care follows a full programme. Morning assembly is held in the school three days each week. Each night Bible reading and prayers are said with the house parents. Scripture Union is held each week. On the Lord's Day all the children attend the Gospel Service in the local church. One Sunday morning while preaching it was a tremendous joy to see seven children stand up and publicly confess to receiving Jesus Christ as their own Saviour. It was also great to see them develop spiritually, being baptised and following the Lord.

Patrick is a fine young man in Grade 8. He has great difficulty in walking even with the use of a stick. His nick name is "the Pastor" because he loves to speak openly about the Lord. He confesses his faith to all the students. Good to see a young evangelist at work! Overcoming his difficulty he never complains and is always smiling.

The children love to sing and some have formed themselves into a choir. They love drama and can perform at an advanced level; in fact the school drama group has represented the province at national level. They especially love to portray scenes of death! Many Bible stories become very vivid through their drama.

The wife of the now deceased President, Mr Levi Mwanawasa, visited the mission. Everyone was greatly excited, especially the children at the school. They were given the privilege and honour of singing and performing drama before her. Her name was Maureen and without any fear of her status they sang the song they had written about "Maureen". The theme of the drama was about the social injustices of the handicapped. Mrs Mwanawasa appeared to enjoy the presentation and entered into the spirit of the occasion.

Because of the generosity of Christians overseas we are able to give a little extra help to the children in the form of clothes and school uniforms. We can also provide a party at Christmas which is a great treat for the children and the staff. Party food usually includes chicken, rice and macaroni. The older girls bake cakes in the Domestic Science department. Then there are the games. These are new to them and have to be learned, and the teachers enjoy them as much as the children.

Annually an exchange is made with Chengelo High School. Now Chengelo is a really top class school for privileged children whilst the Mambilima children come from a very disadvantaged background. A group of our children visits Chengelo for a week. The outdoor activities include canoeing and rock climbing among other things. They achieve skills they never thought possible! On returning, their stories are fantastic. One child was heard to say, "It was great, we all got to wash in a BIG pot!" He was talking about being in the swimming pool! When the Chengelo students come to Mambilima for their exchange week they have great difficulty adjusting the other way. It is a great learning experience for them to see such poverty in the villages.

It is good to know that such vulnerable children are now given the opportunity of holistic care and a sound education. The outlook of their lives is changed. With this education it is possible for them to get suitable work and become integrated and useful members of society.

CHAPTER 14

Brass Tacks

Most of the buildings at Mambilima Mission were old, built with mud bricks and mud plaster. These structures easily become invaded with white ants which climb to the top and eat away the roof timbers. As a result the metal roofing sheets blow off as there is nothing for the nails to grip onto.

There was a desperate need for the school to have a purpose-built building. Brass Tacks was approached for help. Plans were discussed for a square building with an assembly hall in the centre and classrooms built round the outside. All rooms would have wheelchair access. The central hall would be high, open at the top to allow air to circulate. An architect translated these ideas into a blueprint.

Dates were arranged for the team to come during 2004 and a time schedule drawn up. With no need for planning permission we were ready to begin preparations. This involved getting bricks made, collecting sand and stones, digging foundations and buying cement. Soon a team of six men were flown in from the UK to begin the work. The professional men soon corrected the amateurs' attempts at digging foundations!

Local labour was contracted. This included builders, carpenters, electrician, plumber and labourers. Around 30 men were employed. Contracts were agreed which included morning tea and a healthy lunch at close of work. The working day began before dawn - during the day the temperature was sometimes as high as 50°C. To keep an adequate supply of drinking water was a big challenge. It was necessary to get an electrical supply on site which could support all the equipment for the project. ZESCO (Zambian Electric Company) is not known for its speed in making such installations. With some apprehension we approached the manager. He was the sullen, silent type who spoke in monosyllables.

The project was outlined to him and a request made for his help. He was asked when he could do the job. "Get me the material and I will do it tomorrow," he said. A feather could have knocked us over! How often we doubt our Lord's ability. A hurried trip to Mansa procured the required items and true to his word we had an electrical supply on site the next day.

Big stones, small stones and quarried stones were required for the foundations. The mission truck was being used to collect and transport these to the site. On the first Saturday the team finished at lunch time, and then the truck was taken to the farm to collect maize for the hospital. At 3pm news came through to us that the truck had collapsed and died! The engine had seized up. As we sat in the house pondering this disaster, gloom set in. What will we do now? Where will we get a truck quickly enough to get on with the building work?

At 5pm we heard a vehicle entering the compound. What was this? It was a small Toyota Dyna truck which we had bought about six months before. Now having been cleared through customs and registered, the two men decided to deliver it to us from Lusaka this very day! How great is our God! His ways are past finding out! The truck was worth its weight in gold. It worked hard to service the whole project, and is working still!

The local men worked alongside the Brass Tacks team. They were taught many new skills and responded well to the teaching which has turned out to be a great blessing as many new projects since have been entrusted to them. They can be trusted to do a professional job.

When a cement mixer arrived on site, this was something new, no-one had ever seen such a thing. The villagers came to stare at it, their heads going round and round in time with it! It was a great tool. The local men soon learned to use to it and get the mixture and consistency right.

The wood being used was *mukwa* (mahogany). This was a first for the team to make roof trusses with this priceless wood. It was also chosen for the doors and fittings as it resists the attack of white ants.

The Brass Tacks team came from all walks of life. Some were bricklayers, others carpenters and electricians, those from a sales background and an eminent scientist. He was seen in his ill-fitting overalls labelling equipment around the site.

The men slept in the big house on the mission which used to be home to Cathie Arthur, but were fed in our place. But how do you feed six hungry men in a bush village? The Lord knows and supplies what is needed. Bags of lentils, rice and macaroni had just been received in a container sent out from Scotland. Big pots of lentil soup were made each day and disappeared just as quickly as it was made - liked more than Esau liked his pottage!

The men were overheard saying to each other, "At such and such a place they gave us goat to eat." They were actually eating goat regularly and thought it was beef! (Even old Isaac was deceived by a good cook.) One member did not like his meat with gravy, so his meat came out of the pot, the gravy washed off and the portion sizzled in the frying pan for a few minutes. Thus every taste was met, all were satisfied and grateful for the provision.

One of the young fellows was late for supper one night. He had come across a snake. It was a Gabon Viper, beautiful but dangerous. Later it was caught and killed. Some debate took place about keeping the skin. When the villagers heard that the *basungu* were wanting snakes they appeared with one every night for several nights to come – for sale of course!

For a Saturday afternoon a football match was arranged. The local team, called the Panadols would play the Builders. There was great excitement in the village as the match drew near. The team was chosen from those working on the project. It was a tough match but the Builders came out victorious.

Communications with home were a problem. Men away for several weeks missed their families. We had a satellite phone for emergencies - it was a great help but rather expensive. One of the young lads was always wanting his mobile phone taken to Mansa, 60 miles away, where text messages could be sent and received. He said he had to keep in touch with his business. Eventually we discovered his business interest walked on two female legs!

These days were days of real spiritual blessing and effective testimony as the team worked together with each other and the local community. They visited and gave help in several of the local churches, attended a village conference, sampled the local food and enjoyed meeting the believers.

After work they explored the village on foot and bicycle. Some went fishing in dugout canoes on the river, others visited the homes of the local workers. It was great to see how they were accepted into the community. It was a time to be remembered.

The work was completed on time. The manager from ZESCO came to inspect the electrical installation and was impressed by what he saw. True to character he turned to me and said, "Your electrician is a genius," and went on his way.

The new school building is a testimony to the Lord's goodness. It is of great benefit to the children and teaching staff. Today it looks as good as when it was built.

New School Building 2004

CHAPTER 15

The President's Gift

In 1998, Mambilima Mission had its centenary, for in 1898 Dan Crawford had crossed over the Luapula River from what was then Belgian Congo and Zambia's first mission station was established at this very place. So a celebration was arranged, with a conference to be held at a large site on the eastern banks of the river, two miles upstream from Mambilima.

This was shortly after we had moved from Congo into Zambia, so Margaret and I were asked if we would go to Mambilima and host all the visiting guests. Because Mambilima is the oldest CMML Mission, many visitors were expected from around the world as well as from all over Zambia. We agreed and moved into the village.

Our initial residence was in a large, old two-storey house. The facilities were rather limited within the house, and in the loft space bats had taken up residence - the smell was overpowering! However, this situation greatly improved a little later when a family of owls appeared - the bats disappeared.

Some of the visitors from abroad were being flown into Mambilima by a small plane. There is an airstrip at the village. It is rather unusual being about $\frac{3}{4}$ mile long, with tarmac at either end and a dirt track in the centre. The grass along both edges has to be kept short, cut manually with slashers. It is a big job - but the local football team cut it at an agreed cost.

After the airstrip was laid a water system was put into the village. A large metal tank was installed several metres above ground level. Where did they decide to locate it? At the top of the village in direct line of approach to the runway! The pilot has to make sure his approach is spot on. The first time Brass Tacks personnel arrived the plane hit the ground pretty hard and bounced up at least four meters in the air. The pilot quickly took the plane up again and made a smooth landing the next time. They literally did drop in on us!

As the celebration drew near it was better for Margaret and me to move into the smaller house which had somewhat better facilities. We prepared for our guests. Where would they sleep? - as many as possible in the big house, a family on the doorstep in two tents, and some an hour away in Mansa. Soon the beds were in place and ready. Food was bought - maize meal for nshima, rice, fish, goat meat, beef, green vegetables, some tinned food ...

When the first day came, the plane arrived bringing overseas visitors. Former and present missionaries travelled from Mansa. National dignitaries and Government representatives arrived by car. Security was tight. Congo was just on the other side of the river and their civil war was continuing.

The celebration was attended by around 10,000 people from all over Zambia. The name of the Lord was exalted and praised. The Word of God was preached - altogether a great time of rejoicing! The choirs rang out their many anthems. The Government representative was the country's Minister of Religion. He is a fine believer and gave a powerful word of encouragement.

President Chiluba was unable to be with us on the day, but he sent a fine message of greeting. He gifted a large amount of money and granted the whole of this large site to CMML. What a blessing this has been.

Now it was lunch time. All the missionaries and dignitaries arrived at the house, over thirty were present. Food appeared from various sources. The table was laden - everyone was filled and satisfied. Outside a posse of solders and guards waited expectantly. There was enough and to spare to feed these hungry men as well. The Lord can still provide to feed a multitude!

The celebration lasted four or five days, the Lord supplying our needs daily. It was a wonderful time of fellowship. The last day was a day of relaxation. An outing was arranged to Mumbalumba Falls, a local beauty spot on a safe river with a fine bathing area. After swimming and some good fun a picnic lunch brought a grand finale. The Lord was thanked sincerely and we went our separate ways.

At this conference site, the Luapula Provincial Conference is now held every two years. Around 10,000 still attend, coming from far and wide. It is held in the dry season with no risk of rain. The believers walk for miles, cycle, come on crowded lorries or in coaches. All bring their *katunda* (goods and chattels). They are here for a week, it is their holiday. Some live in tents, but most make booths from grass or reeds, and segregate areas for themselves for the week. Congregating in their different local church groups the ladies cook, the men debate and the choirs sing. The camp is wakened at 5am with a hymn and prayers and closes down at 11pm with evening prayers.

Each day there are three teaching sessions, and in the evening the Gospel is preached. Each session is interspersed with choirs singing their praises to God.

The preaching desk is built under a huge overhanging rock. It really is huge and oval shaped, about ten metres in diameter and four metres high, perched on a base about three metres wide. This gives shade to those underneath its rim and a secure foundation underfoot. It is good to be under the shadow of a mighty rock! The psalmist said also that God had lifted him out of a horrible pit and "placed his feet on a rock".

Preaching under the "Mighty Rock"

The large congregation sits on the ground in a vast semicircle around the rock-shaded preaching point. Recent developments have seen wooden poles cemented into the ground on top of which reed mats are placed to give some shade from the fierce heat of the sun. Now some permanent seating is also being organised.

On the Lord's Day morning the Lord's Supper is held. Around 4,000 believers will break bread. Thirty loaves of bread are bought and several litres of red juice prepared. It is a solemn occasion and carried through very reverently. A time of open worship and thanksgiving takes place. Those taking part will use the microphone so that they can be heard.

At an appropriate time, the deacons come forward and take the broken bread to different parts of the large congregation. The same is repeated for the cup - many cups are required. While some are partaking the rest of the congregation will quietly and worshipfully sing appropriate hymns. A great sense of reverence is experienced while the Lord Jesus is remembered.

Believers Gathering for Conference 2008

Recently two accommodation blocks with ten rooms in each have been built. Toilet and ablution blocks are also now in place. Two large water tanks and a water system have been installed, with water pumped up from the river to supply the needs of the people. The site is being developed and well used for the glory of God and the benefit of many of His people.

Dust fills the air in the dry season at the conference, often needing to be dampened down. Although the folks are here for a whole week it is amazing how the ladies especially can turn out each day so immaculately dressed, clean, tidy and colourful, as if from a "band box".

The local marketeers cash in on the opportunity during the conference. The road to the site is lined with dozens of makeshift stalls. One can buy anything – bread, vegetables, fish, live chickens, oil, matches ... it is even possible to have your mobile phone charged!

Such a time of rejoicing, protracted celebration, and living under the sky, reminds me of the Jewish Feast of Tabernacles, with the people living in their "booths". It is also easy to see how the Lord Jesus at the age of twelve was left behind in the temple among the crowds during another such celebration.

This conference meets a great need in the province. Isolated Christians can enjoy the company of others and the Word of God is explained by capable teachers. This is not the case in every village church. We praise the Lord for such a provision.

CHAPTER 16

Personalities

In the villages there are many who stand out as quite unique personalities. For some of them it is because they have a mental weakness or illness. In rural areas the treatment of those with mental illness leaves room for much improvement. Many have mental problems as a result of taking drugs or alcohol, often made locally with no control of purity or strength.

Frank is a tall well-built man who wanders around the village all day. He speaks the most beautiful English. It is said he had been in the army and for some reason he was beaten. His mental weakness may be one of the results of this.

One day while we were speaking with each other he said, "You *basungu* are different from us." "Only in the colour of our skin," I replied. "No!" he said. "How are we different?" I asked. "You think differently," he replied. He had grasped the fact of a cultural difference between us!

I asked why he did not go and cultivate a garden. "You are a big strong man - you could grow vegetables." Indignantly he replied, "I am an intellectual! Intellectuals don't garden!" I told him that the school teachers and the doctor did gardening. He replied, "They are not intellectuals, but I am!" It is so sad to see big strong men just walking around begging for food!

Same Same was employed as a night watchman. He was a very amenable man and very helpful until he was drunk! Why is he called Same Same? was asked one day - because you always find him the same each day with a big smile on his face, was the reply!

There was a period some years ago when the Congolese came across the river with guns and raided the village. A party of Zambian soldiers were sent to guard the village. They arrived late one night and were billeted in the house Same Same was guarding. In the morning he appeared to hand in his watchman's torch. "Did you go home and leave the soldiers?" we asked. "No," he said, "I stayed at my post and guarded the soldiers!"

Zana is well known in the village. He is always a great source of information. He lived with his sister who kept him clean and well fed. In return he did a little gardening for her. Other than that he just wandered about the village. His brother had joined the army, trained as a mechanic and had done well for himself. He keeps in touch with Zana and sends clothes for him from time to time.

How Zana got his information was unreal. The stories he told appeared so outlandish but they usually turned out to be true. His favourite greeting was, "The Bible for Zambia. Zambia needs the Bible." Then he would give a rendering of John 3.16. There seemed to be nothing he did not know. One day coming out of the bookshop he met Margaret. "The driver of the late Noeline Stockdale is hiding from you in the bookshop," he said. This man had a "*mulandu*" (an unresolved matter) which he did not want to face up to. He had seen Margaret coming and had gone to take refuge in the back of the shop. But his ploy was blown as Zana had spotted him!

Mwali was another who came around the house. His spoken

English was good but he made a nuisance of himself around the village. He would take drugs and alcohol and become cantankerous. Margaret worked with him and he would do some work outside the house. The villagers marvelled that he would work for anyone. He wanted to come to church but needed a Bible. His clothes were little better than rags so needed a shirt and trousers to be presentable, he said. It is amazing how people want to be presentable to come into the presence of God. This appears to be the case in every culture. Is this because of a feeling of guilt in the presence of holiness? The believers coming to the meetings are always clean and tidy although never overdressed.

Kankomba Elliot was an old elder in the village church, a wise old man whose conversations on spiritual matters we often enjoyed. On one occasion a suit of clothes arrived in a parcel from the UK and we decided it would fit the old man. We sent it to him, and a letter of thanks was received with a note which said, "If we had a shirt and tie it would look good with the suit." Well, we found these and sent them to his house. Again a note returned saying, "Thank you, and all I need to look good is a pair of socks and shoes!" Amazingly they too were found and delivered. Again the note of thanks and the letter - it said, "Sometimes it gets very cold and if possible a coat would finish the outfit." God is so good. We found a coat and sent it to him.

Some time later, motoring through a nearby village we came across a funeral being held by the roadside. There was old Kankomba standing in the midst of the crowd. He was preaching the Word of God complete with suit and overcoat under the blazing heat of the sun! If you have clothes you do need to let them be seen!

Abel Kataya was a boy of around four years old when he started coming to the house. Bert and Isobel Cargill were with us at the time and he wormed his way into their hearts.

When Isobel asked his name his reply sounded like "Eckyboki". This name has stuck with him. He was a likable lad who had an answer for everything. Wherever you turned he was at your heels. He would run errands and deliver notes wherever you wanted even though he was so young. His father was dead and he lived with his mother and siblings in the village. They were very poor and we often gave them a little food and some clothing for which his mother was truly grateful.

Kataya went to the local village school but appeared to be learning nothing. It is sad to see how little learning actually takes place in some of these schools. There are classes of fifty; one class taught in the morning and another in the afternoon, and often the teacher is absent. Kataya had no real interest in learning. But this boy has ability and it needs to be harnessed. Taking him under our wing he was moved into the school for the handicapped where we trust he will be able to fulfil his potential. There is so much potential in these villages if only it could be released and realised.

William is our night watchman, a man you can depend on, being a very stable man with a good Christian testimony. He gathers with another church in the village. He is the fount of all knowledge and knows all that is happening in the area. When waiting for a particular vehicle to arrive and you hear a noise, you ask William if this is it. He will tell you yes or no with accuracy, and if no, will tell you to whom it belongs.

One day the message came to us that there had been a murder in the part of the village where William lived. It was a mob murder. When William came on duty that night we requested an explanation of what happened.
"Well," he said, "the murdered fellow was stealing goats."
"But is that a reason for murder?" we asked.
"He was warned many times but would not stop," he said.
"He won't steal anymore goats now!" and the conversation finished!!

Grasping the ways and peculiarities of individuals is a most challenging experience in any culture. During these days at Mambilima we were entering into the lives of many different people, and God was using them to teach us important lessons in life.

CHAPTER 17

Bibles and Books

In Zambia there is a real hunger for literature to read especially by middle-aged and younger people who have recently learned to read English. The official language of Zambia is English, used in all Government business - Police, Immigration and Education. Potentially therefore in the country there is access to a wealth of written material.

Some newspapers are available, all in English, but they are costly. This makes them unavailable to most people in the rural villages. If someone does get a paper it is passed round several households and read by many before it falls to pieces.

A number of different local languages are spoken by the various tribal groups. Bemba or Chibemba is the largest of these and is spoken and understood from the Democratic Republic of Congo in the north right through Zambia to villages in the south of the country.

The Bemba Bible was translated from the original languages in stages. Dan Crawford translated the Gospels of the New Testament. His original handwritten scripts are held in Edinburgh by the Bible Society. In addition Willie Lammond and George Sims both worked on the New Testament and Psalms. *Icipingo na Masamo* (New Testament and Psalms) was published in the 1920s.

The British and Foreign Bible Society (BFBS) recognized that this New Testament represented "Western Bemba". Meanwhile (Rev) McMinn and (Rev) Paul Mushindo of the Church of Scotland were working in the Northern Province, on the eastern side of the Bemba-speaking area. They produced an initial draft of the whole Bible. The Bible Society realised that some of this "Eastern Bemba" would not be widely understood in the Luapula Province farther west.

So in 1938 the BFBS called on Mr Lesley G Barham to work with McMinn and Mushindo to produce a Bible which could readily be used by all Bemba speakers. (Mr L G Barham is the father of Ray Barham who has been serving the Lord at Mansa for many years.) McMinn retired after some years, but Mushindo and Barham with other consultants continued until 1955 when the work was completed. During those 17 years Mr Barham had typed through the Bemba manuscripts three times on a portable typewriter! The "*Baible*" was produced in 1956.

Over the years, the supply of these Bibles has been rather erratic because of cash flow difficulties at the Zambian Bible Society. However Mr Geoff Rushton of Opal Trust has negotiated the printing of these in Korea, and now there is a steady uptake of Bibles throughout the country.

This Bible is not a reference Bible which is a disadvantage to many who wish to study the Scriptures. To help in this area Mr Alan Park has produced a Bemba Concordance. It is not exhaustive but it is a great help in studying the Word. At a two-day seminar with elders, time was devoted to showing them how to use such a tool. It is easy for us to forget that this is something completely new to these elders who speak only Bemba.

The Bible Society of Zambia had in its possession a set of audio tapes of the Bemba New Testament. There was potential in these to provide the Word of God to the many people who still cannot read, or for the benefit of those who are blind. So permission was given to use these tapes to produce multiple copies of the New Testament in spoken format on a solar powered i-pod. The material was transferred onto CDs and then sent to Megavoice in Tiberias, Israel where the i-pods were produced.

I-pod New Testament at Bookstall

The first quantity of these i-pods was taken to Mambilima during the 2008 regional conference where they were at once in great demand. Being solar powered they are very convenient and cost effective to use. (Batteries are expensive and last only a short time.) They can be used by individuals or by a church. They can also be used to improve reading skills and pronunciation for public speakers because the quality of the Bemba is excellent. Although rather more expensive to produce than paper-based materials, there is great potential in this technology.

Giving out Christian literature is easy but can present difficulties. On one occasion we were surrounded by such a large crowd that it was frightening with everyone desperately trying to get hold of something to read. Setting up a bookstall in the market square was better and always drew large crowds. These were always happy times mixing with the people, and many constructive discussions took place about eternal matters.

It was our habit to carry a good supply of literature in our vehicle wherever we went. Booklets like "Our Daily Bread" and others were very suitable for this purpose. There are many road blocks in Zambia, manned by either Police, Army, or Immigration officers. They usually accept literature thankfully, are very polite, and start reading immediately. As we were leaving one such road block one day an army officer came running after us shouting, "My parents, my parents!" We stopped. "Thank you for the booklet you gave me when I was on duty at the bridge. I read it and trusted the Lord Jesus as my Saviour. Oh thank you, thank you!" he said. He had been baptised and was fellowshipping in a local church. "Cast your bread upon the waters, for you shall find it after many days," says the Word of God (Eccl 11.1).

Another day we were stopped by a policeman. Offering him a booklet he said, "It's not this I want, it's a BBC." What is this, we thought, does he want a radio? No - he went on to explain it was a MacDonald's "Believer's Bible Commentary" he was requesting. He was a believer in one of the local churches! Well we could get one for him, but we did not carry these large books around with us to give away.

There is another group of people who flood the valley with highly attractive, multicoloured booklets, both in English and in Bemba. They come from the Watchtower Press. They are very appealing to the local people, and we find many believers carrying them in their hands as they come to the services in many churches. Unfortunately these local believers often cannot differentiate between what is true and what is false.

Children are in abundance everywhere you go. It is important to reach out to them. Most churches do hold regular Sunday Schools but they have little or nothing in the way of visual aids to assist in their teaching. So we have supplied charts, pictures and flannelgraphs and these have been a great help. But what assistance has been given appears to be like a drop in a bucket, the need is so vast.

To encourage the children a small gift can sometimes be given to them. Some of our supporters from overseas take the time to prepare such gifts, for example attaching a pen or a pencil to a used picture/text card. To receive just a pencil is a great thing for these children, and the card is also valued. It will be displayed in their house all year.

Another avenue of service to the local believers has been to hold seminars for Sunday School teachers in various centres. We teach them how to use the basic resources that they have around them, and try to widen their teaching methods to go beyond rote learning. We show them how to use different strategies and visual aids in their teaching, and teach them how they can develop learning through play. This is a very new idea to them – how to play with children!

In one church a young man was trying his own novel idea to get the children to memorise Bible verses. A prize was being offered for having memorised the verses. It was a box of matches! - a very useful prize! Then the adults in the congregation were challenged to say where the particular verse was found in the Bible. If they were correct they too got a box of matches! This brother was using his initiative and his own money!

Wind-up tape recorders have been useful in the past. These are used with a set of tapes and flip charts. The teaching is in Bemba and using a prompt to turn the chart, the story is told. This is a most useful method for adults as well as children. As technology develops it may be possible to introduce other similar methods of spreading the Word of God, such as the i-pods referred to above.

The Bible is the living Word of God, bringing life wherever it is received. It is sharper than a two-edged sword. It changes lives whenever it is believed. This chapter describes a most important aspect of our ministry in Zambia.

Books and Tapes for Distribution

CHAPTER 18

Disappointments

Life is full of ups and downs, highs and lows, encouragements and disappointments. It is great to experience times of rejoicing, but at times the soft south wind is exchanged for the cold north blast. It is so very sad to see those you love, and those on whom you have expended much energy in their spiritual life, let the Lord down and turn from the ways of God. Here is the story of some of them. *Their names have been changed to protect their identity.*

Noah was a brilliant young man. He came to work at the hospital and was sponsored to take a course in pharmacy. Every exam he sat, he passed with distinction. However, in his final exam he was given a 'fail' in pharmacy. This was not at all expected. Repeating his last year again the college actually used him to teach pharmacy! But again he failed the pharmacy exam. Challenging the college principal, we accused the department with corruption. "He won't fail the next time," they promised, and made him retake the exam which he passed. Sadly such situations are discovered time and time again!

Taking up an appointment at Mambilima hospital he gave his all to the work. In the church he was preaching and being a great help. Then he started to drink alcohol. Within weeks he was a wreck. Much time and effort was spent collecting him in his drunken stupor as he raved he was the "chosen one". His old father, a godly elder, was heartbroken. Many hours were spent counselling but to no avail. Much prayer was made around the world for Noah. Eventually he was dismissed.

Some years later the phone rang at home in Scotland. It was Noah. He had repented and was restored to the Lord. He was now married and had a family of two girls. There was great rejoicing that he had returned. The Lord taught us the important lesson never to give up praying!

Caleb was the hospital administrator when we arrived at Mambilima. He was a local boy with limited education who had worked himself into the position he held. But on joining the hospital board of management we were discovering irregularities. It was difficult to find what was the actual problem. Money appeared to be misused, drugs and other items were going missing. Wages were being calculated so that senior employees were receiving more than they should. No accurate record was kept of staff holidays or attendance on duty. The administration was in free-fall.

The problem pointed in one direction but it was difficult to prove. The staff closed ranks and would not speak about the matter. During these days it was good to have the support of the Divisional Nursing Officer who was a member of a local church and a member of the local hospital board.

It was reported that Caleb had committed adultery. As a result he was removed from the fellowship of the local church. This also meant that he had to be removed from his position of hospital administrator. These were sad days as we walked through this valley!

But Caleb has repented of his ways and has returned to the Lord. He is back in church fellowship. His lovely family visit our home from time to time giving us the opportunity to give them some help with their education.

Meshek was a very dear friend with whom we spent a lot of time. He had a lovely wife and family of two boys and two girls. Meshek was given the post of head teacher of the school for the handicapped children. Working well with the staff the school moved forward.

Later we noticed that Meshek was not coming to see us as often as he used to. It was reported he was visiting the home of a female teacher. The children could see this and when asked if they knew where the Head was they said, "The sir is with the madam." This was proved to be correct. Much counselling and help was given to try and save the situation but the position deteriorated. His wife was no longer able to live with him and she went back to her own village.

Following the correct procedure, Meshek was moved to another school. There has been no repentance. He now lives in that district with the other girl and has another family, although he supports his original family in their schooling. Such situations are heartbreaking and emotionally draining.

There was a young man working in the dental department of the hospital. He was a bright young fellow and was sponsored to take a dental course. The contract stated that on completion he would give two years' service at the hospital. However on completion of his course he refused to return. This was most disappointing as he was a Christian and in church fellowship.

Many boys were helped with sponsorship of their education. *Daniel* was a very bright young man. He completed his nurse education with distinction. But he could look you straight in the eye and tell you an outright lie - a situation that arises time and again. He said he was going to the Christian Union while training, but that was a lie, he had gone to meet with another group!

Students who were being sponsored were expected to do some work at the mission during the school holidays. Two of these boys were reported to be stealing from our garage. We checked but could see nothing amiss. Another boy one day came to the house wearing an overcoat. "Where did you get this?" we asked. "I bought it in the village and it was stolen from your garage - but you won't believe me," he said.

The matter was reported to the police. They searched the house in the village where the coat had been bought. "It was like a shop," they said, "everything laid out for sale." The boys were brought to our home by the police, protesting their innocence. After some softening up by the police they confessed and showed us how they broke into the garage. Removing screws from two hinges, one of them squeezed himself into the garage. He then carefully slit open the cartons and removed clothes from each box and passed them to his friend. This took place during lunch break.

They were taken to the cells and then to court and given a prison sentence. Many times we saw them out cutting grass in the fierce sun under the watchful eye of a prison officer and an AK47! Later, visiting the Electricity Board offices next door to the prison I was aware of two boys running to me calling my name. It was these same two lads. They had completed their sentence and were just released. They wanted me to give them a lift back to Mambilima. There was no shame, no repentance. They expected life just to begin again where it had left off!

Another fellow worked with us as a plumber. He had worked along with the Brass Tack team and was good at his work. He continued to work at the mission as required. One day he was arrested by the police. To our horror we found that he was accused of molesting young girls. It was investigated, he was charged and taken to the High Court. The outcome was a long sentence and to the present day he is still inside.

As we go through dark valleys, even the valley of death, the Lord is with us. His rod and staff comfort us. We have known His intimate company in many such situations during our service for Him. Haven't you, my reader, found that too?

Epilogue

As you have travelled with us through these pages we trust that you have found this journey a pleasant one. We would like it to be God's hand that has been seen as we have moved into various towns, villages and communities.

When we think back over the last 70 years or more we can see the great change which the Lordship of Jesus Christ has made in the lives of many people. When Dan Crawford arrived in the area there were no Christians there at all. Now in the Luapula province of Zambia there are around 400 churches under the name of Christian Brethren or Christian Missions in Many Lands (CMML). There are also many other followers of the Lord Jesus Christ who meet in other groups.

The then paramount Chief, Mwata Kazembe, resisted Crawford and his teaching. He said to him about Christianity, "You live with us for 25 years and we will see the difference that Christianity makes - and then we will accept your message."

What a change today! The present chief, a grandson of the one Crawford dealt with, is surrounded in his district with many churches of Christians. He has lost much of his power. One day we gave this little man, dressed in a western-style suit, a lift in our vehicle as we travelled to Kashikishi. Our conversation was very open and free but as far as we know he has still not accepted Jesus Christ into his life.

It has recently been observed by a journalist who is a confessed atheist that where Jesus Christ has been accepted in African communities a real change has occurred. He wrote this:

"I've become convinced of the enormous contribution that Christian evangelism makes in Africa: sharply distinct from the work of secular NGOs, government projects and international aid efforts. These alone will not do. Education and training alone will not do. In Africa Christianity changes people's hearts. It brings a spiritual transformation. The rebirth is real. The change is good."

Later:

"Whenever we entered a territory worked by missionaries, we had to acknowledge that something changed in the faces of the people we passed and spoke to: something in their eyes, the way they approached you direct, man-to-man, without looking down or away." [1]

During our time in Congo and Zambia it has been our joy to be accepted in churches, homes and communities. Even such reserved people as both Bembas and Scots have thrown their arms around each other's necks – and shared a kiss of welcome!

Truly our Lord's promise has been fulfilled to us, "You shall go out with joy and be led forth with peace."

[1] Matthew Parris, *The Times*, 27 Dec 2008

Bibliography

This is a brief selection of books which can give more information and additional background to the missionary work described in this short book.

Barham, R. *Remember your Leaders – Imitate their Faith,* 40 pages. (Messages given at the Christian Brethren (CMML) Centenary Conference 24th August 1998) African Christian Books, P.O. Box 90376, Luanshya, Zambia, 1998.

Mutenda, Kovina L.K. *A History of Christian Brethren in Zambia,* 198 pages. Christian Resource Centre, P.O. Box 11235, Chingola, Zambia, 2002.

Crawford, Dan *Thinking Black,* 485 pages. Morgan and Scott Ltd, 12 Paternoster Buildings, E.C. London, 1912. Reprinted by John Ritchie Ltd., Kilmarnock, 2009.

Crawford, Dan *Back to the Long Grass, My Link with Livingstone,* 373 pages. Hodder and Stoughton Ltd, London.

Ellis, James J. *Dan Crawford of Luanza,* 160 pages. John Ritchie, Kilmarnock, Scotland.

Stunt, W.T. *Turning the World Upside Down,* 661 pages. Upperton Press, Upperton Gardens, Eastbourne, Sussex, 1972.

Tatford, Fredk. A. *Light Over the Dark Continent,* 547 pages. Echoes Publications, 1 Widcombe Crescent, Bath, Avon, 1984.